An Anthology of Modern Italian Poetry

An Anthology of Modern Italian Poetry

In English Translation,
with Italian Text

Edited and translated by
Ned Condini

Introduction and notes by
Dana Renga

The Modern Language Association of America
New York   2009

© 2009 by The Modern Language Association of America
All rights reserved. Printed in the United States of America

MLA and the MODERN LANGUAGE ASSOCIATION are
trademarks owned by the Modern Language Association of America.

For information about obtaining permission to reprint material from
MLA book publications, send your request by
mail (see address below) or e-mail (permissions@mla.org).

Library of Congress Cataloging-in-Publication Data

An anthology of modern Italian poetry in English translation,
with Italian text / edited and translated by Ned Condini;
introduction and notes by Dana Renga. pages cm. — (Texts
and translations ; 25) Includes bibliographical references.
ISBN 978-1-60329-032-6 (pbk. : alk. paper)
1. Italian poetry—20th century—Translations into English.
2. Italian poetry—20th century.   I. Condini, Ned, 1940- .
PQ4225.E8C66 2009
851'.908—dc22   2008043931

Texts and Translations 25
ISSN 1079-252x
ISSN 1079-2538

Pages 429–31, containing copyright notices and acknowledgments
for permission to reprint the Italian poems and translate them,
constitute an extension of the copyright page.

Cover illustration of the paperback edition: sketch by Piero Lerda. Torino,
Italy, 1954. Untitled. A gift from Piero Lerda to Ned Condini

Third printing 2020

Published by The Modern Language Association of America
85 Broad Street, suite 500, New York, New York 10004-2434
www.mla.org

I know no surgery of the heart that can
lay it bare, unscramble its meaning.
Grace perhaps (I often think of it—
not much peace in that), but it, too, rare
and instant as a bolt of lightning.

Yet fire is present; it seems to be all.

—M. Luzi

CONTENTS

The Lyrical Poets

The Hermeticists

The Neo-Avant-Garde

Contemporary Poets

INTRODUCTION

It is no easier to contextualize the poetic landscape of modern Italy than it is to translate a line of verse. Often categorized as a succession of various isms—decadentism, futurism, and hermeticism, to name a few—Italian poetry of the last hundred years is far from homogeneous. Successive genres and movements were repeatedly at odds with one another, the rapport between poets was frequently contentious, and poems provided battlefields for the intelligentsia. Moreover, many movements existed simultaneously, embodying competing ideologies, styles, or conceits. Italy was unified in 1870, and its post-Unification history is complex and at times controversial, filled with economic, political, and social tensions. Modern and contemporary Italian art, literature, and cinema frequently engage these tensions, and the selection of poems in this anthology must also.

Anthologizing the poetic tradition involves making choices, at times difficult ones, about which poets, poems, and movements to represent. Indeed, only a few recent anthologies in Italian have been truly comprehensive, including, for example, a selection of woman poets (Amelia Rosselli is among the most frequently anthologized), covering the major literary movements from the fin de siècle (approximately the last twenty years of the nineteenth century) to the present day, and containing not only authors and works with a firm place in the Italian literary canon but also lesser-known poets and poems. The modern Italian poets in this anthology, some of whom are translated into English for the first time, offer a more extended look at post-Unification Italian culture. Reflected in their poems are many of the philosophical, ethical, political, and social concerns that characterize the last hundred and thirty years.

Italy toward the end of the nineteenth century was far from unified, and the new state was forced to come to terms with a fractured nation. It faced many pressing social issues, including the *questione meridionale* ("southern question"), female emancipation, intense regionalism, severe poverty, and the growing power of the mafia. Writers such as Luigi Capuana (1839–1915), Matilde Serao (1865–1927), and Giovanni Verga (1840–1922) directly engaged many of these problems in that venue of prose fiction known as verismo, an Italian version of realism inspired by French naturalism and based on positivism or on the philosophical belief spearheaded by Auguste Comte (1798–1857) that the world can be better known through scientific inquiry and empiricism than through speculation or subjective experience. In an aesthetic indebted to Aristotelian mimesis, many of the *veristi* believed that by objective exposition social problems could be known, understood, and therefore rectified.

Other members of the Italian intelligentsia during the fin de siècle were at a loss with this method. Instead of putting their trust in science, industry, and emerging technologies, they invented new idioms to express the crisis of modernity. Many writers, in particular Gabriele D'Annunzio, looked toward the French symbolists for a literary model, especially Stéphane Mallarmé (1842–98), Paul Verlaine (1844–96), and Arthur Rimbaud (1854–91), who had broken with traditional forms of expression. The symbolists wrote of sensorial derangement, of the unknown and the bizarre in a highly allegorical, metaphoric language. They shared a mistrust for the realistic aspects of language, desiring instead to forge new connections between the subject and the world, recasting the poet, as in Rimbaud's influential "Letter to Paul Demeny," as a "voyant" ("seer"), "par un long, immense et raisonné *dérèglement* de *tous les sens* (251; "by a long, immense, and rational derangement of all of the senses" [my trans.]). Their poems, consequently, were hermetic and their idioms sonorous and replete with unconventional syntax.

Two forerunners to twentieth-century Italian verse, both influenced by the French symbolists, open this anthology: Giovanni Pascoli and D'Annunzio. Spanning the two centuries, Pascoli and D'Annunzio are cornerstone poets, positioned as figures for others to emulate, debate, and surpass. Many successive poets are referred to as "dannunziani" and "anti-dannunziani," for example. Although different thematically and stylistically, both Pascoli and D'Annunzio expressed many of the quagmires of the new Italy. Both treated such disparate themes as militarism and budding socialism. Unlike the so-called last of the nineteenth-century poets, Giosuè Carducci (1835–1907), whose poetic comprehension followed the rules of science, Pascoli and D'Annunzio refuted objective truths, proffering more personal and instinctive experiences.

Pascoli's poetry embodies what critics have come to call a "poesia delle cose" ("poetry of things"), in which logical thought processes are suppressed and mood is evoked through a complex analogical system. In "Patria" ("Homeland"), Pascoli recalls a dream of a summer day through a series of emotionally charged sensory images ("tremulo di cicale" ["whirring cicadas"], "l'*angelus* argentino" ["silvery vespers"]). Such refined poetic flashes both heighten the expressive quality of the object-image and introduce pervasive thematic concerns: in this case, grief and nostalgia; elsewhere, death, pain, and misfortune. In a landscape of industrialization and personal trauma, Pascoli's poetic subject often appears alienated and estranged; images in the present recall irretrievable relationships and experiences. In the poetic treatise "Il fanciullino" ("The Young Child"), Pascoli attributes a restorative function to poetry. By getting in touch with their inner child, poets write of the mystery inherent in life and death in a verse style that is spontaneous and, above all, instinctual. True poetry, he argues, is discovered and not invented. Like Carl Jung, Pascoli believed in a collective unconscious or universal psyche that connects all forms of life.

D'Annunzio, frequently referred to as the Italian decadent poet par excellence, believed that life should be experienced as an artistic phenomenon. He felt the cult of beauty and aestheticism to be more pressing than social responsibilities; his celebrated amorality and *superomismo* ("cult of the superman") allowed him none of the social concerns common in Pascoli's poetics. For D'Annunzio, poetry is allegorical for lived experience, as he makes clear in his novel *Il piacere* ("The Child of Pleasure"): "Il verso è tutto. Nell'imitazione della Natura nessuno istrumento d'arte è più vivo, agile, acuto, vario, multiforme, plastico, obbediente, sensibile, fedele (149; "Verse is everything. In imitating Nature, no other artistic instrument is more alive, agile, acute, varied, multiform, plastic, obedient, sensitive, faithful"). Ultimately abandoning positivism, D'Annunzio considered the new prophet to be the poet, not the scientist. His poems are decidedly melodic, and devices such as anaphora, assonance, internal rhyme, alliteration, and enjambment evoke poetically charged mise-en-scènes (e.g., a pine wood, a sweltering noon day, an olive grove). Like the French symbolists, he stretched the boundaries of language and frequently combined terms belonging to dissimilar sensorial camps, as when he writes in his celebrated "La pioggia nel pineto" ("Rain in the Pine Wood") of "parole più nuove / che parlano gocciole e foglie / lontane" ("new words uttered by leaves / and the distant droplets of rain").

While many of D'Annunzio's verses and novels praised militarism, a subversive voice to the bellicose and colonial position of the new Italy can be found in Gian Pietro Lucini's (1867–1914) free-verse poetry. Lucini's satirical "La canzone del giovane eroe" ("The Song of the Young Hero") criticizes colonial projects in Abyssinia and Eritrea; it also critically assesses many of the aspirations of the ruling elite. His "young hero" or "Campione dell'italianità" ("champion of Italianness") is a bourgeois and corrupt capitalist. Driven by his anarchist sensibilities, Lucini rebelled against conventional metrics and had a polemical stance against D'Annunzio (made clear in his *Antidannunziana* of 1914). In many of his poems, he employs irony to unveil the tragic duplicities of life. "La canzone della cortigianetta" ("The Song of the Young Courtesan") is both "giocondo" ("joyful") and "arrochito" ("harsh"), as her makeup and other fineries only mask her "nostalgie inutili, / le reticenze, le angoscie, le pazzie, / e desideri vani e le impossibili malinconie" ("vain nostalgia, / reticence, madness, pain, / fruitless pursuits, overwhelming despair").

Corrado Govoni (1884–1965) and Aldo Palazzeschi (1885–1974) prefigure both the futurist and twilight (or crepuscular) movements. Although they had ties to each group at various points in their careers, their participation was marginal. But no matter how Govoni is categorized, his poetry is based on instinct. His position in the Italian poetic tradition is polemical: although he credits himself with founding crepuscularism, his work does not fit neatly into any one movement. His earlier, symbolic verse falls into the category of liberty or art deco—distinguished by emphatically descriptive verses—but a predominant melancholic link with humble objects aligns him with the crepuscular poets, though irony, a conceit common to many poets of that movement, is rare in his work. A penchant for the visual, in poems primarily from 1911 to 1915, puts him with the futurists. Object images are central to much of his work. In investigating the multifaceted nature intrinsic to most things, Govoni foregrounds the underlying sense of detachment that characterizes Italy at the beginning of the century.

Palazzeschi renamed the poet *saltimbanco* ("mountebank"), and his earlier verses are typified by a radically experimental style, which he often uses to criticize his predecessors (such as Carducci and D'Annunzio). Palazzeschi participated in the futurist movement, yet in 1914 he publicly and quite vehemently detached himself from it. His humorous, combustible verses focused on the moment, rejecting any sort of melancholic rapport with the past. His poetic subject frequently ridicules moral standards. In particular, his *L'incendiario* (1910; "The Incendiary") is an attempt to set fire to, through a subtle use of irony that aligns him with the twilight poets, antiquated social norms. Logic has no place in his poetry. He undermines traditional syntax and highlights purely instinctual situations (the sexual act, flashes of madness), in this way breaking free from the prison house of language and linguistic tradition.

Sergio Corazzini (1886–1907), Guido Gozzano (1883–1916), and Fausto Maria Martini (1886–1931) are three of a group of poets who participated in the first attempt to conceive of a poetic movement in early-twentieth-century Italy. The name *twilight*, evoking the melancholy of early evening, was applied to the group retrospectively in 1910, in an unfavorable article by Giuseppe Antonio Borgese. Although the group was by no means a school, the poems of the twilight poets shared a common ethos. Pain, grief, and imminent death set their work apart. Many suffered serious illnesses: Corazzini and Gozzano both died young of tuberculosis. Martini was severely wounded during World War I. Decomposing things, common in their verse, externalize the physical breakdown occurring both in their bodies and in the natural world, and their preoccupation with death often takes the form of elegies to simple, defunct, or unused objects and creatures. Dusty villas, overgrown gardens, dead flowers, and broken bottles are evoked in a straightforward and unassuming language, in opposition to the excessive rhetoric and aestheticism of Carducci, D'Annunzio, or even Pascoli.

Common in the work of the twilight poets is a melancholic relation with the past, repeatedly shown to be irretrievable, and the steady use of irony. Through subtle contrasts between present and past, they express their existential predicament and alienation. Resignation in the face of suffering and despair makes them antithetical to D'Annunzio's triumphant lyricism. Anticipating Eugenio Montale's (1896–1981) dialectics of negativity, the crepuscular poets express their weariness and disillusionment with the world. In Corazzini's "Desolazione del povero poeta sentimentale" ("Desolation of the Poor Sentimental Poet"), a quintessential poem of the movement, the narrator declares, "Io non sono un poeta. / Io non sono che un piccolo fanciullo che piange" ("I'm not a poet. / I'm nothing but a little boy who cries"), who wants to die "solamente, perché sono stanco" ("only because I'm tired"). In a similar vein, Gozzano ends his well-known poem "La Signorina Felicita ovvero la Felicità" ("Miss Felicity") by articulating the irreconcilable disjuncture between the invented or imagined self and its present-day reality, as he is "Quello che fingo d'essere e non sono!" ("What I pretend to be and am not!"). Even grief is fruitless, as made clear in Martini's "San Saba," one of many poems dedicated to Corazzini, in which cypresses, traditional funereal trees, are "brancolanti come ciechi" ("groping like blind men") and stand before a church, San Saba, which is described as a "tempio al suicida" ("shrine to suicide").

The regressive and nostalgic twilight poets find their antipode in the verse of the futurists. Unlike the vaguely defined group of twilight writers, futurism was unequivocally founded on 20 February 1909, when Filippo Tommaso Marinetti (1876–1944) published the notorious "Fondazione e manifesto del futurismo" ("The Founding and Manifesto of Futurism") on the front page of the French newspaper *Le figaro*. As is clear in the name of the movement, Marinetti called for a revolution against the past. All literary and social traditions (including libraries, museums, and academies—institutions Marinetti labeled "cemeteries") must be eradicated in order to focus on the future. The manifesto was a call to arms, and its glorification of war, the machine, and speed is resonant with protofascist sentiments played out in two subsequent wars. In short, Marinetti promulgated a new idea of beauty, one stripped of any nostalgia or connection with nature and aligned instead with violence, misogyny, and the mechanization of human life. The futurists actively lived their beliefs, hosting outlandish "serate futuriste" ("futurist evenings") complete with futurist recipes, plays, and dress.

The futurists ultimately rejected the symbolic trend in Italian poetry that typified fin de siècle verse. Marinetti's natural target was D'Annunzio, and Marinetti attacked his predecessor's propensity for depicting natural landscapes embedded with nostalgic sentiment. His "Manifesto tecnico della letteratura futurista" ("1912; "Technical Manifesto of Futurist Literature") spelled out the futurists' dictum "Parole in libertà" ("Words in Freedom") or an essentially free-verse, visual style. Punctuation, adverbs, adjectives, and a psychological subjectivity were to be abolished in favor of an instinctual, chaotic technique. In their attack on institutions and conventional thought, the poets, writers, visual artists, and critics that made up futurism—members included Umberto Boccioni (1882–1916),

Carlo Carrà (1881–1966), Valentine de Saint-Point (1875–1953), and Giacomo Balla (1871–1958)—prefigured many twentieth-century avant-garde movements, including surrealism and dadaism.

While the futurists tended to ignore social realities, focusing instead on propelling Italy to the forefront of European modernism, several contemporary literary journals, such as *Leonardo* (1903–07), *La voce* (1908–14; "The Voice"; published from 1914 to 1916 as *La voce letteraria* ["The Literary Voice"]), and *Lacerba* (1913–15), all based in Florence, promoted a return to social awareness and responsibility. Of these three periodicals, *La voce* contributed most profoundly to the intellectual and cultural climate in Italy in the years leading up to World War I. Founded by Giuseppe Prezzolini in 1908 (who in 1903 had cofounded *Leonardo* with Giovanni Papini, which called for a return to pragmatism), *La voce* was primarily concerned with cultural renewal in modern aesthetics. The publication became a forum for poets, writers, critics, philosophers, and economists to debate the crises of the day—whether social, ethical, political, artistic, spiritual, or existential.

The poets in this anthology who contributed to the review are Camillo Sbarbaro (1888–1967) and Arturo Onofri (1885–1928). Much of their verse took the form of the lyrical fragment, or an unstructured, instinctual verse style, which F. J. Jones calls "lyrical *veggenza* ['clairvoyance']" (69), a term undoubtedly indebted to Rimbaud. The literary movement to which many of these writers belonged (including Sbarbaro and Onofri) is known as *frammentismo* or fragmentism and implies both a writing style—many verses are presented in the form of understated, lyrical

flashes—and subject matter: the *frammenti* ("fragments")
generally present autonomous pieces of the physical and
natural world instead of depicting integral experiences
or objects (Pascoli is an example). The poetry of *La voce*,
then, gives voice to the incomplete and detached meta-
physical condition characteristic of the prewar years. Po-
ets writing in this disconnected manner utilize analogy
in presenting splinters of life and forging new connec-
tions between disparate entities or sensations. In Onofri's
verse, for example, March is a season that "mette nuvole
a soqquadro" ("dismembers clouds") and is likened to "un
fanciullo in ozio, a cavalcioni / sul vento che separa due
stagioni" ("an idle kid, astride / the wind parting two sea-
sons"). In confronting traditional aesthetic attitudes, the
vociani ("*Voice*-ists") addressed penetrating social issues,
including spiritual dilemmas (Onofri), social injustice, and
existential and psychological angst (Sbarbaro).

Some of Italy's most renowned poets of this century—
Umberto Saba (1883–1953), Giuseppe Ungaretti (1888–
1970), and Eugenio Montale—belong to an ill-defined
genre entitled *i lirici nuovi* ("the new lyricists"). They are
grouped together in this anthology as "the lyrical poets"
(typically, the label was given in retrospect, by Luciano
Anceschi). Common themes characterize the verses of the
lyrical poets—I have also included Vincenzo Cardarelli
(1887–1959), Maria Luisa Spaziani (1924–), and Antonia
Pozzi (1912–38)—many of whom are concerned with time
(memory, the seasons, and commemoration are frequent
tropes), grief, and trauma. Several of these poets are civi-
cally engaged. Ungaretti recalls the distressing experience
of World War I in *L'allegria* ("Happiness"), and poems such
as "Soldati" ("Soldiers") and "Veglia" ("Keeping Vigil")

are poignant attempts literally to breathe life back into the bodies of his lifeless companions. Montale, in "Dora Markus" and "La primavera hitleriana" ("Hitler's Spring"), eloquently expresses his antifascism. So does Spaziani, who, in *Donne in poesia* (1992; "Women in Poetry")—a collection of twenty imaginary interviews with female poets, including Pozzi—restores voice and vision to a group of seminal woman writers. Conversely, Cardarelli is frequently criticized for being too focused on lyrical classicism (one of the key values of the literary journal *La ronda,* which he founded in 1919) and for ignoring the sociopolitical climate of early fascism.

This group of writers often gives speech to humble or marginal events and creatures (particularly Saba and Montale). This characteristic simultaneously aligns them with and distinguishes them from the crepuscular poets: their opaque verses are regressive and ironic but by no means as nihilistic as those of the *crepuscolari.* Moreover, they do see a revitalizing aspect to poetry. Saba catalogs the many subtleties of his native Trieste (its inhabitants, neighborhoods, and interludes) in a formal and lucid style. Montale, in recalling ordinary, diurnal particulars— among his many talismans are lemons and eels—foregrounds the present-tense locus of memory. The two female poets placed under this rubric view poetry as potentially restorative. In poems such as "Il destino" ("Destiny") and "Preghiera alla poesia" ("Prayer to Poetry") Spaziani and Pozzi, respectively, posit that, through writing and remembering, grief and suffering might be provisionally alleviated (Pozzi committed suicide when she was only twenty-six). The new lyricists, in particular Saba, Cardarelli, Ungaretti, and Pozzi (each of whom wrote one poem entitled "Nostalgia"), are keenly interested in the aesthetics of homecoming, and much of their poetry envisions a painful return—to refer to the etymology of nostalgia itself—to a past identity that has been irretrievably lost.

The lyrical poets are quite frequently fused (and confused) with the hermetic poets, no doubt because both groups use a hermetic language, best described as orphic and somewhat impenetrable. Although poets such as Ungaretti, Montale, Spaziani, and Pozzi do at times fit under the umbrella of hermeticism, the poetry of the new lyricists is overall quite diverse and distinctive. Like the new lyricists, the hermeticists were far from unified. The name for the movement was given in retrospect, in 1936 by Francesco Flora, who wrote in *La poesia ermetica* ("Hermetic Poetry"), disparagingly, of Ungaretti's abstruse poetic language.

Many of the poets represented in this section of this volume wrote in the style of hermeticism (e.g., privileging the unknown over the known, the natural over the artificial), yet it is difficult to align any one of them unilaterally with the movement. The early verse of Salvatore Quasimodo (1901–68), Mario Luzi (1914–), Vittorio Sereni (1913–83), and even Andrea Zanzotto (1921–) has in common technical characteristics (repetition, little or no punctuation, empty spaces on the page, lucid syntax or analogy) and thematic concerns (death, grief, nostalgia, memory, natural landscapes, the poetic voyage). Through such stylistic and topical foci, the hermetic poets strip meaning from language, laying words bare on the page, ultimately underlining the isolated, inert subject position of the poetic narrator. Many, including Sandro Penna (1906–77), Giorgio

Caproni (1912–90), Cristina Campo (1923–77), and Roberto Sanesi (1930–2001) are set apart in their earlier poetry by a keen interest in memorializing landscapes. Nostalgia and subjectivity frequently color both bucolic and urban milieus (settings treated include the Sicilian countryside, winter wastelands, and abandoned factories). Two of the poets who appear here (Luzi and Campo) are keenly interested in such religious motifs as mysticism and redemption.

A frequent criticism of the hermetic poets was that they were too introspective, so focused on individual experience that they ignored social realities. The destructive experience of World War II combined with over twenty years of a fascist dictatorship in Italy redirected the attention of many of these poets. The later poetry of Quasimodo, Luzi, Sereni, Caproni, Campo, and certainly Zanzotto is ethically, politically, socially, and environmentally engaged. In this way, these poets find a space in which to address Theodor Adorno's well-cited dictum regarding the efficacy, or even the possibility, of writing poetry after the Holocaust (34). After the war, for example, Quasimodo underwent a radical shift; declaring hermeticism a thing of the past, he wrote *Giorno dopo giorno* (1947; "Day after Day"), a text that recalls the atrocities of the war while articulating a hopeful outlook for the future of Italy.

Apparent in postwar poetry, literature, and cinema is the attempt to ground aesthetics in historical practice, redirecting focus away from individual experience and toward collective struggle. Although neorealism is best known as a cinematic style (key neorealist directors are Roberto Rossellini, Vittorio De Sica, and Luchino Visconti), it was also the genre writers chose to express the crisis of the postwar years. Based on French naturalism and Italian verismo, the goal of neorealism was to wed history with myth and the imagination, ultimately promoting social awareness. New art must be engaged, many argued, in order to continue to address the numerous social, political, and economic crises of the postwar years. Some major concerns were the growing divide between economic classes, the exploitation of the poor, regional prejudice, and a conservative and corrupt government. Several of the poets included under the classification of realistic experimentation are ideologically grounded. This grouping does not connote a clearly defined school or movement but is defined instead by shared concerns and stylistic choices; it contains Franco Fortini (1917–94), Rocco Scotellaro (1923–53), Elio Pagliarani (1927–), Pier Paolo Pasolini (1922–75), Amelia Rosselli (1930–96), and to some extent Carlo Betocchi (1899–1986) and Alfredo de Palchi (1926–). Many of these poets, Marxists or socialists, contributed to politically committed journals and dailies such as *Ragionamenti* ("Reasonings"), *Comunità* ("Community"), and *Avanti!* ("Go Ahead!"). Perhaps the most influential and controversial was Pasolini, a Marxist, homosexual, and Catholic. An active Communist, Pasolini was expelled from the party for indecent behavior and subjected to countless obscenity trials from the 1950s until his violent and unsolved murder in 1975. In his pivotal poem "Le ceneri di Gramsci" ("Gramsci's Ashes"), the narrator visits Antonio Gramsci's grave in Rome. (Gramsci, a hero of the new left, was imprisoned under fascism for eleven years until his death in 1937. His influential *Lettere dal carcere* [*Prison Notebooks*] is a vehement attack on cultural hegemony.)

Sibilla Aleramo (1876–1960), Amalia Guglielminetti (1881–1941), and Rossana Ombres (1931–) were all, to various degrees, involved with Italian women's movements in the twentieth century and keenly interested in writing women's lives, thereby inscribing the female subject into a traditionally masculine culture. Although Aleramo and Guglielminetti wrote before the period of new realism, they share several thematic concerns and attitudes with later writers: the interconnectedness of art and life, a critical assessment of gender attitudes, the communal position of women, to name a few. Many of these women are socially committed. Aleramo was involved with the women's and workers' movements in the early 1900s, and Guiducci was aligned with the feminist movement of the 1960s and 1970s.

Pagliarani and Rosselli, two of the poets categorized under realistic experimentation, were decisively involved with the Italian neo-avant-garde, a movement unambiguously launched in 1961 with the publication of *I Novissimi: Poesia per gli anni '60* (ed. Giuliani; "The Newest Poets: Poetry for the Sixties"). In addition to Pagliarani, four other poets—Alfredo Giuliani (1924–), Edoardo Sanguineti (1930–), Nanni Balestrini (1935–), and Antonio Porta (1935–89)—were included in the volume. A significant moment for the neo-avant-garde came in 1963, when a substantial group of poets, novelists, and theorists convened in Palermo and formed Gruppo 63. These and other writers were reacting against both the disenchantment of the postwar years (despite the ethical impulse of engaged art, social, economic, and political conditions grew increasingly worse in Italy) and the so-called neo-crepuscularism that colored the poetry of that period—

a term coined by Giuliani to describe the contemporary tendency to flee reality through verse. Their poems, consequently, attempted to show the world as it was—chaotic, antagonistic, fragmented—instead of how it might be imagined or idealized. In his introduction to *I Novissimi*, Giuliani puts forward two unifying aspects to the poems in the anthology: "una reale 'riduzione dell'io'" (21; "a real 'reduction of the I' "), which recalls Marinetti's "Technical Manifesto of Futurist Literature," and a style with no trace of decadence or self-indulgence. Through formal experimentation—neologisms, lack of punctuation, multilingualism, fractured syntax—the group aimed to simultaneously shock and estrange the reader, bringing to the foreground the schizophrenic nature of contemporary culture.

The modern poets that close this anthology are too thematically and stylistically diverse to be put into any one genre or movement. In addition, several are just beginning their careers as poets and are still developing. They do all seem to be, in the words of Anna Malfaiera (1926–96), "al grado zero" ("at ground zero," translated in this anthology as "at zero level"), in that these poets— with Luigi Fontanella (1940–), Milo De Angelis (1951–), Valerio Magrelli (1957–), and Giorgio Guglielmino (1957–)—return to a more direct, uncomplicated style instead of relying on forms and techniques handed down by their predecessors.

These poets advance fresh perspectives on many aspects of Italian culture. In his discussions of ethnicity and difference, Fontanella questions if genuine multiculturalism is possible in Italy or America. Magrelli continues the compelling discourse on gender identity begun in the twentieth century. Overall, the poets suggest a more fluid, nomadic approach to gendered subjects, clear in Magrelli's "Ho finalmente imparato..." ("At last I've learned..."), in which the narrator finally is taught to read "la viva / costellazione delle donne / e degli uomini" ("the live / constellation of women and men") as disordered yet unified. In response to the feeling of emptiness that so characterizes the media age, De Angelis nostalgically searches out childhood memories through the 8mm film, while the poems of Malfaiera's *Il più considerevole* ("The Most Considerable") remind the reader of precarious human relations and herald the violence of the next decade.

In an aesthetic indebted to Saba, Montale, or Spaziani, many of these poets describe simple objects, events, or natural forms. They also delicately address, through discussing the minute, many present-day issues. With subtle images of fishermen, a long jump, or the details of a kitchen, these poets hark back to a less media-driven society and contest the alienating effects of postmodernity. In the end, they realize the interconnectedness of art and life and understand that the word can (quite literally in Guglielmino's visual poetry) break free from the page.

Far from overcoming antiquated attitudes about gender, ethnicity, and regionalism, Italy today gives the impression of reverting to sexual, ethnic, and regional stereotyping. In their treatment of ethnicity, gender, politics, the media, and aesthetic production, the poets that close this anthology arrive at a sensibility that is nomadic and non-hierarchical, suitable to a climate that is labile socially, sexually, economically, and politically. In response to the many struggles that Italy faces in the new millennium (intense xenophobia, continued gender inequity, a media-driven government), the poets that close this anthology, though by no means as politically engaged as the new realists, continue to contest the status quo.

Acknowledgments by Ned Condini

I thank the Italian Cultural Institute in New York for its encouragement and support. I am indebted to E. Sanguineti, both for some biographical information and for the organization of my anthology, which derives from his *Poesia italiana del Novecento* (Turin: Einaudi, 1971).

My thanks to Marilyn, whose untiring, pointed, and creative collaboration has been a work of love.

Works Cited

Adorno, Theodor. "Cultural Criticism and Society." *Prisms*. Trans. Samuel Weber and Shierry Weber. Cambridge: MIT P, 1967. 17–34. Print.

D'Annunzio, Gabriele. *Prose di romanzi*. Roma: Mondadori, 1988. Print.

Giuliani, Alfredo, ed. *I Novissimi: Poesia per gli anni '60*. Torino: Einaudi, 1965. Print.

Jones, Frederic J. *The Modern Italian Lyric*. Cardiff: U of Wales P, 1986. Print.

Pascoli, Giovanni. *Poesie: Il fanciullino*. Milan: Fabbri, 1970. Print.

Rimbaud, Arthur. *Œuvres complètes*. Paris: Gallimard, 1972. Print.

SUGGESTIONS FOR FURTHER READING

Ammirati, Maria Pia, and Ornella Palumbo, eds. *Femminile plurale: Voci della poesia italiana dal 1968 al 2002*. Catanzaro: Abramo, 2003. Print.

Ballerini, Luigi, ed. *Shearsmen of Sorts: Italian Poetry, 1975–1993*. Stony Brook: Center for Italian Studies, Stony Brook U, 1992. Print.

Ballerini, Luigi, Beppe Cavatorta, Elena Coda, and Paul Vangelisti, eds. *The Promised Land: Italian Poetry after 1975: A Bilingual Edition*. Los Angeles: Sun and Moon, 1999. Print.

Bàrberi Squarotti, Giorgio. *La cultura e la poesia italiana del dopoguerra*. Bologna: Cappelli, 1966. Print.

Baroni, Raouletta, and Piero Cigada, eds. *La poesia italiana del Novecento*. Milano: Vallardi, 2000. Print.

Blum, Cinzia Sartini, and Lara Trubowitz, eds. *Contemporary Italian Women Poets: A Bilingual Anthology*. New York: Italica, 2001. Print.

Condini, Ned. "Mystical Carnality in de Palchi's *Paradigma*." *Italian Quarterly* 43.167–68 (2006): 71–82. Print.

Feldman, Ruth, and Brian Swann, eds. *Italian Poetry Today: Currents and Trends*. New York: New Rivers, 1979. Print.

Frabotta, Biancamaria, ed. *Donne in poesia: Antologia della poesia femminile in Italia dal dopoguerra a oggi*. Roma: Savelli, 1977. Print.

———. *Italian Women Poets*. Toronto: Guernica, 2002. Print.

Gentili, Alessandro, and Catherine O'Brien, eds. *The Green Flame: Contemporary Italian Poetry with English Translations.* Dublin: Irish Academic, 1987. Print.

Gioia, Dana, and Michael Palma, eds. *New Italian Poets.* Brownsville: Story Line, 1991. Print.

Lind, Levi Robert, ed. *Twentieth-Century Italian Poetry: A Bilingual Anthology.* Indianapolis: Bobbs, 1974. Print.

Loi, Franco, and Davide Rondoni. *Il pensiero dominante: Poesia italiana, 1970-2000.* Milano: Garzanti, 2001. Print.

Lorenzina, Niva, ed. *Poesia del Novecento italiano: Dalle avanguardie storiche alla seconda guerra mondiale.* Roma: Carocci, 2004. Print.

Marchione, Margherita, ed. *Twentieth-Century Italian Poetry: A Bilingual Anthology.* Rutherford: Fairleigh Dickinson UP, 1974. Print.

McKendrick, Jamie, ed. *The Faber Book of Twentieth-Century Italian Poems.* London: Faber, 2004. Print.

Mengaldo, Pier Vincenzo. *Poeti italiani del Novecento.* Milano: Mondadori, 2000. Print.

O'Brien, Catherine, ed. *Italian Women Poets of the Twentieth Century.* Dublin: Irish Academic, 1996. Print.

Picchione, John, ed. *The New Avant-Garde in Italy: Theoretical Debate and Poetic Practices.* Toronto: U of Toronto P, 2004. Print.

Picchione, John, and Lawrence R. Smith, eds. *Twentieth-Century Italian Poetry: An Anthology.* Toronto: U of Toronto P, 1993. Print.

Porta, Antonio, ed. *Poesia degli anni settanta.* Milano: Feltrinelli, 1979. Print.

Sanguineti, Edoardo. *Poesia italiana del Novecento.* Torino: Einaudi, 1971. Print.

Smith, Lawrence R., ed. *The New Italian Poetry, 1945 to the Present: A Bilingual Anthology.* Berkeley: U of California P, 1980. Print.

Spatola, Adriano, and Paul Vangelisti, eds. *Italian Poetry, 1960–1980: From Neo to Post Avant-Garde.* San Francisco: Red Hill, 1982. Print.

Viazzi, Glauco. *Dal simbolismo al deco.* Torino: Einaudi, 1981. Print.

Vitello, Ciro, ed. *Antologia della poesia italiana contemporanea, 1980–2001.* Napoli: Pironti, 2003. Print.

An Anthology of Modern Italian Poetry

Fin de Siècle

GIOVANNI PASCOLI

Giovanni Pascoli was born in San Mauro di Romagna in 1855 and died in Bologna in 1912 from cirrhosis of the liver. His life was marked by loss: in 1867 his father was murdered, the next year his mother and sister died, and four other siblings died soon afterward. Pascoli was a pacifist, and death and consolation are common themes of many of his poems, such as "Agonia di madre" ("A Mother's Agony") and "X agosto" ("August Tenth"). In 1879, he was briefly jailed for his involvement with an anarchist group; this experience prompted him to give up politics and return to academia. *Myricae,* his first and best-known collection of poems, was published in 1890. His other major publications are *Primi poemetti* (1904; "First Poems"), *Canti di Castelvecchio* (1903 and 1912; "Songs of Castelvecchio"), and *Nuovi poemetti* (1909; "New Poems"). His poetry is often bucolic, focused on the lower classes and simple living things (such as the humble tamarisk or "Myricae"). He believed that poets should maintain their capacity for wonder by viewing the world through the eyes of the uncorrupted child or *fanciullino.*

Patria

Sogno d'un dì d'estate.

Quanto scampanellare
tremulo di cicale!
Stridule pel filare
moveva il maestrale
le foglie accartocciate.

Scendea tra gli olmi il sole
in fascie polverose;
eran in ciel due sole
nuvole, tenui, róse:
due bianche spennellate
in tutto il ciel turchino.

Siepi di melograno,
fratte di tamerice,
il palpito lontano
d'una trebbïatrice,
l'*angelus* argentino...

dov'ero? Le campane
mi dissero dov'ero,
piangendo, mentre un cane
latrava al forestiero,
che andava a capo chino.

Homeland

Dream of a summer day.

Such a tremulous play
of whirring cicadas!
The mistral drove
curled-up leaves strident
down the row.

The sun streamed through the elms
in bands of beams; the sky
held two clouds only,
˙tenuous, eaten away:
two dabs of white
in the cobalt-blue sky.

Pomegranate hedges,
bushes of tamarisk,[1]
the hidden throbbing
of a threshing machine,
silvery vespers . . . Where

was I? The bells told me
where I was, weeping, while
a dog barked at the stranger
walking by, his head bowed.[2]

---

[1] Pascoli's favorite shrub, the tamarisk, also named myricae, has scalelike leaves and pink flowers. See Sanguineti, *Poesia italiana del Novecento* (Torino: Einaudi, 1971) 9.

[2] From the dreamed-of homeland the poet is brought back to the reality of exile.

L'assiuolo

Dov'era la luna? ché il cielo
notava in un'alba di perla,
ed ergersi il mandorlo e il melo
parevano a meglio vederla.
Venivano soffi di lampi
da un nero di nubi laggiù;
veniva una voce dai campi:
chiù...

Le stelle lucevano rare
tra mezzo alla nebbia di latte:
sentivo il cullare del mare
sentivo un fru fru tra le fratte;
sentivo nel cuore un sussulto,
com'eco d'un grido che fu.
Sonava lontano il singulto:
chiù...

Su tutte le lucide vette
tremava un sospiro di vento;
squassavano le cavallette
finissimi sistri d'argento
(tintinni a invisibili porte
che forse non s'aprono più?...);
e c'era quel pianto di morte...
chiù...

The Horned Owl

Where was the moon? For the sky
was swimming in a pearly dawn,
and the almond and apple trees
strained to see it on tiptoe.
Puffs of lightning did shoot
from black clouds far below;
from the fields rose a call:
hoot, hoot.

Scattered stars were twinkling
in that milky mist:
I heard the sea's lullaby
and a rustling in the twigs;
I felt a wincing in the heart
like the echo of a bygone cry.
Far away sobs broke out:
hoot, hoot.

On each shimmering peak
a breath of wind was trembling;
the grasshoppers were shaking
thin silver tambourines
(jinglings at unseen doors
that will open no more?);
and still that dirge-like toot—
hoot, hoot . . .

Digitale purpurea

I

Siedono. L'una guarda l'altra. L'una
esile e bionda, semplice di vesti
e di sguardi; ma l'altra, esile e bruna,

l'altra... I due occhi semplici e modesti
fissano gli altri due ch'ardono. «E mai
non ci tornasti?» «Mai!» «Non le vedesti

più?» «Non più, cara.» «Io sì: ci ritornai;
e le rividi le mie bianche suore,
e li rivissi i dolci anni che sai;

quei piccoli anni così dolci al cuore...»
L'altra sorrise. «E di': non lo ricordi
quell'orto chiuso? i rovi con le more?

i ginepri tra cui zirlano i tordi?
i bussi amari? quel segreto canto
misterïoso, con quel fior, *fior di*...?»

«*morte*: sì, cara.» «Ed era vero? Tanto
io ci credeva che non mai, Rachele,
sarei passata al triste fiore accanto.

Foxglove

I

They are seated, one gazing at the other.

One's blond and slender, plain in dress and looks;

but the other, dark and slender, the other one . . .

The shy, naive eyes stare

at the fiery ones. "You never went

back?" "Never!" "You never saw the nuns again?"

"Never, my dear." "I did. I went back, saw

my white nuns and relived

the tender years you know;

those childhood years so precious to the heart."

The other smiled. "And say: don't you remember

the fenced-in garden? the berries in the brambles?

juniper bushes where the thrushes chirp?

the bitter boxwood? that uncanny, secret

song with a flower in it, *flower of* . . . ?"

"*Death*: yes, dear." "And was it true? I so much

believed it that I would have never, Rachel,

never gone near that melancholy flower.

According to Maria Pascoli, the poet's sister, the poem is indebted to a story she told
Giovanni about her convent stay at Sogliano. It is considered to be a meditation on
the problem of evil.

Ché si diceva: il fiore ha come un miele

che inebria l'aria; un suo vapor che bagna

l'anima d'un oblio dolce e crudele.

Oh! quel convento in mezzo alla montagna

cerulea!» Maria parla: una mano

posa su quella della sua compagna;

e l'una e l'altra guardano lontano.

II

Vedono. Sorge nell'azzurro intenso

del ciel di maggio il loro monastero,

pieno di litanie, pieno d'incenso.

Vedono; e si profuma il lor pensiero

d'odor di rose e di viole a ciocche,

di sentor d'innocenza e di mistero.

E negli orecchi ronzano, alle bocche

salgono melodie, dimenticate,

là, da tastiere appena appena tocche...

Oh! quale vi sorrise oggi, alle grate,

ospite caro? onde più rosse e liete

tornaste alle sonanti camerate

For it was said: the flower holds a honey
that stuns the air, a perfume of its own
that bathes the soul in sweet, cruel oblivion.

That convent nestled in the azure mountain!"
Mary recalls. One of her hands
rests on the hands of her companion:

and each avoids the other's eyes.

II

They see. There rises in May's peacock sky
their convent, full
of litanies and incense.

They see: their thoughts take on the scent
of roses and violets in clusters:
a smell of mystery and innocence.

Forgotten melodies ring in their ears,
rise to their lips from keyboards over there
brushed upon barely . . .

Oh! what dear guest smiled at you at the grating
today? and flushed and happier you returned
to echoing dorms today: and today *Ave*,

oggi: ed oggi, più alto, *Ave*, ripete,

Ave Maria, la vostra voce in coro;

e poi d'un tratto (perché mai?) piangete...

Piangono, un poco, nel tramonto d'oro,

senza perché. Quante fanciulle sono

nell'orto, bianco qua e là di loro!

Bianco e ciarliero. Ad or ad or, col suono

di vele al vento, vengono. Rimane

qualcuna, e legge in un suo libro buono.

In disparte da loro, agili e sane,

una spiga di fiori, anzi di dita

spruzzolate di sangue, dita umane,

l'alito ignoto spande di sua vita.

III

«Maria!» «Rachele!» Un poco più le mani

si premono. In quell'ora hanno veduto

la fanciullezza, i cari anni lontani.

Memorie (l'una sa dell'altra al muto

premere) dolci, come è triste e pio

il lontanar d'un ultimo saluto!

Ave Maria your voice at choir louder

repeats; and then all of a sudden

you burst out crying. Why?

They weep a little, in the golden sunset,

without a reason. So many girls are standing

in the garden, here and there brightened by them.

Brightened and buzzing. The girls come in spurts,

sails in the wind. Some stay

and read the good book they have brought.

Apart from them, agile and healthy,

a spike of flowers, fingers rather, sprinkled

with blood, a human's fingers,

sends out the hidden breath of its life.

III

"Mary!" "Rachel!" Their hands squeeze each other

a little tighter. They have just seen childhood,

the distant, cherished years.

Dear memories (that one has of the other

by merely pressing), how solemn and heartrending

echoes the fading of a last farewell!

«Maria!» «Rachele!» Questa piange, «Addio!»
dice tra sé, poi volta la parola
grave a Maria, ma i neri occhi no: «Io,—

mormora,—sì: sentii quel fiore. Sola
ero con le cetonie verdi. Il vento
portava odor di rose e di viole a

ciocche. Nel cuore, il languido fermento
d'un sogno che notturno arse e che s'era
all'alba, nell'ignara anima, spento.

Maria, ricordo quella grave sera.
L'aria soffiava luce di baleni
silenzïosi. M'inoltrai leggiera,

cauta, su per i molli terrapieni
erbosi. I piedi mi tenea la folta
erba. Sorridi? E dirmi sentia: Vieni!

Vieni! E fu molta la dolcezza! molta!
tanta, che, vedi... (l'altra lo stupore
alza degli occhi, e vede ora, ed ascolta

con un suo lungo brivido...) si muore!»

"Mary!" "Rachel!" The latter cries. "Good-bye!"
she then says to herself; then turning her
grave words, not her dark eyes, to Mary: "I,"

she murmurs, "did. Alone with the green beetles
I smelled that flower. The wind carried a scent
of roses and violets in clusters.

In my heart lay the languorous turmoil
of a dream that at night flared, at dawn
faded instead in the unconscious soul.

Mary, I remember that ominous night.
The air was laced with silent thunderbolts.
I moved in gingerly,

cautiously, up the soft velvety banks.
The thick grass housed my feet. You're smiling . . . And
I heard a voice that said: Come! Oh, do come!

And all of it so unbearably sweet!
So much so that . . . see (now the other glances
over amazed, and understands, and listens

with a long shudder) you can die of it."

GABRIELE D'ANNUNZIO

Gabriele D'Annunzio was born in Pescara in 1863 and published his first book of poetry, *Primo vere* ("Time of Spring"), at the age of sixteen. Engaged in politics, he was elected to parliament (on the extreme right) in 1897, and in 1919 he occupied Fiume with a group of legionnaires to protest the allocation of Dalmatia to Yugoslavia. In 1921, he shut himself off from the world in his decadent Vittoriale, in Gardone sul Garda, until his death in 1938 of a cerebral hemorrhage. D'Annunzio was very prolific, writing poems, novels, and plays, and is recognized for the poetry of his *Laudi del cielo del mare della terra e degli eroi* ("Lauds of Sky and Sea and Earth and Heroes"), which includes *Maia* (1903), *Elettra* (1903), and *Alcyone* (1903); for his novels in the *Romanzi della Rosa* ("Novels of the Rose"), which are *Il piacere* (1889; "The Child of Pleasure"), *L'innocente* (1891; "The Innocent"), and *Il trionfo della morte* (1894; "Triumph of Death"); and for plays such as *La figlia di Iorio* (1903; "Iorio's Daughter"). His poetry, frequently set in charged natural settings and described as decadent, is rhythmical and highly symbolic and often addresses such themes as intuition, the cult of aestheticism, and the Nietzschean superman.

Il sollazzo

Io veggo le mie belle in un verziere,
come nel fresco dell'Orcagna, al sole
splendere ghirlandate di viole;
e attender quivi ognuna al suo piacere.

E non, come le antiche, uno sparviere
avere in pugno né toccar viole.
Sparger fiori talune; altre, parole;
altre volgere un lor dolce pensiere.

Dal vertice di un albero la Morte
contemplarle; ed al suo sguardo sfiorire
le monde carni floride in su l'ossa.

Io veggo le mie belle tremar forte,
sfiorire, illividire, irrigidire;
e coricarsi ognuna in una fossa.

Fiddling Away

I see my beauties glowing in a garden
as in Orcagna's painting,[1] in the sun
each crowned with violets and each
tending to her own fun.

Very unlike those of old, none of them plays
a viola or holds a hawk in hand.
Some toss flowers about, some bandy mots,
some muse on dainty thoughts.

I see Death look at them from a treetop,
and at his glance their clean, esculent flesh
lose color on their bones.

I see my beauties tremble in despair,
drained of life, livid, turning rigid,
and each one lays herself down in a tomb.

---

[1] *The Triumph of Death*

La pioggia nel pineto

Taci. Su le soglie
del bosco non odo
parole che dici
umane; ma odo
parole più nuove
che parlano gocciole e foglie
lontane.
Ascolta. Piove
dalle nuvole sparse.
Piove su le tamerici
salmastre ed arse,
piove su i pini
scagliosi ed irti,
piove su i mirti
divini,
su le ginestre fulgenti
di fiori accolti,
su i ginepri folti
di coccole aulenti,
piove su i nostri volti
silvani,
piove su le nostre mani
ignude,
su i nostri vestimenti
leggieri,

Rain in the Pine Wood

Hush. On the fringe
of the forest I hear
no human words that you speak;
I receive
new words uttered by leaves
and the distant droplets of rain.
Listen! It rains
from the scattered clouds,
it rains on the tamarisks'
salt-parched shroud,
it rains on the pines
scaled and steep,
it rains on the myrtles divine,
on the sage flashing
with blossoms close-mustered,
on the junipers clustered
with berries fair-scented,
it rains
on our sylvan faces,
it rains on our bare hands,
it rains on the cool

su i freschi pensieri

che l'anima schiude

novella,

su la favola bella

che ieri

t'illuse, che oggi m'illude,

o Ermione.

Odi? La pioggia cade

su la solitaria

verdura

con un crepitío che dura

e varia nell'aria

secondo le fronde

più rade, men rade.

Ascolta. Risponde

al pianto il canto

delle cicale

che il pianto australe

non impaura,

né il ciel cinerino.

E il pino

ha un suono, e il mirto

altro suono, e il ginepro

altro ancora, stromenti

diversi

sotto innumerevoli dita.

thoughts that our soul

newly disclosed,

on the dear old romance

that charmed you yesterday,

that today

holds me in trance,

O Hermione.[1]

Do you hear? Rain falling

on the solitary green

starts a crackling

that carries and varies

rumbling thick, humming thin.

Hear! The cicadas' song

contrapunts the lament

and the riotous skies rouse no fears.

And the pine has one sound,

the myrtle one sound,

the juniper its own other sound:

chords vibrating diverse

under fingers newfound.

---

[1] Hermione is the daughter of Helen of Troy.

E immersi
noi siam nello spirto
silvestre,
d'arborea vita viventi;
e il tuo volto ebro
è molle di pioggia
come una foglia,
e le tue chiome
auliscono come
le chiare ginestre,
o creatura terrestre
che hai nome
Ermione.

Ascolta, ascolta. L'accordo
delle aeree cicale
a poco a poco
più sordo
si fa sotto il pianto
che cresce;
ma un canto vi si mesce
più roco
che di laggiù sale,
dall'umida ombra remota.
Più sordo e più fioco
s'allenta, si spegne.
Solo una nota

And immersed here we lie

in the forestal breath,

with arboreal

life palpitating,

and your rapt face is wet

like a rain-sopped leaf,

and your hair's perfumed

like the glowing sage,

earthly child

whom I call

Hermione.

Hear, oh hear! The airy cicadas' song

grows dull while the plaintive flow's

more profuse;

but new notes rise and fuse:

raucous rune

from the darkness,

moist darkness

remote.

Now much fainter, the tune

quavers low, fades away.

A lone note

ancor trema, si spegne.

Non s'ode voce del mare.

Or s'ode su tutta la fronda

crosciare

l'argentea pioggia

che monda,

il croscio che varia

secondo la fronda

più folta, men folta.

Ascolta.

La figlia dell'aria

è muta; ma la figlia

del limo lontana,

la rana,

canta nell'ombra più fonda,

chi sa dove, chi sa dove!

E piove su le tue ciglia,

Ermione.

Piove su le tue ciglia nere

sì che par tu pianga

ma di piacere; non bianca

ma quasi fatta virente,

par da scorza tu esca.

E tutta la vita è in noi fresca

aulente,

undulates, fades away,

quivers long,

dies away.

No more's heard the sound of the sea . . .

only drops on the foliage,

the silvery tears

that cleanse, just the changeful rampage

on the thick-growing sprig,

on the branch bulging thick.

Hush! Mute

is the child

of the air;[2] but the child

of the far bog,

the frog,

sings in the gloomier bushes,

who knows where, who knows where!

And it rains on your lashes,

Hermione.

It rains on your lashes dark,

as though wild you cried

yet with joy; not white,

but as if green with life you had sprung

out of the bark.

Existence lies

cool and perfumed,

_____

[2] The child of the air is the cicada.

il cuor nel petto è come pesca

intatta,

tra le palpebre gli occhi

son come polle tra l'erbe,

i denti negli alveoli

son come mandorle acerbe.

E andiam di fratta in fratta,

or congiunti or disciolti

(e il verde vigor rude

ci allaccia i mallèoli

c'intrica i ginocchi)

chi sa dove, chi sa dove!

E piove su i nostri volti

silvani,

piove su le nostre mani

ignude,

su i nostri vestimenti

leggieri,

su i freschi pensieri

che l'anima schiude

novella,

su la favola bella

che ieri

m'illuse, che oggi t'illude,

o Ermione.

in our breast the heart
is a peach unplucked;
under eyelids your eyes
are like springs in a glade,
and your teeth
almonds out of the skin.
And through brambles we dart
now entwined, now apart
(as the green undergrowth
tugs so hard at our ankles
and our knees are entangled)
who knows where, who knows where!

And there's rain
on our sylvan faces,
rain on the cool
thoughts that our soul
newly disclosed,
on the dear old romance
that charmed me yesterday, that today
holds your mind in a trance,
Hermione.

Free Verse

GIAN PIETRO LUCINI

Born in Milan in 1867, Gian Pietro Lucini is considered a precursor to futurism. He suffered from tuberculosis since childhood, lost a leg to the disease in his youth, and finally died from the malady in Breglia in 1914. He graduated with a degree in law in 1890 and was an outspoken critic of the government. Lucini is best known for his novel *Gian Pietro da Core* (1895) and collections of poetry such as *Il libro delle Figurazioni Ideali* (1894; "The Book of Ideal Representations"), *Revolverate* (1908; "Revolver Shots"), and *Canzoni amare* (1909; "Bitter Songs"). He spelled out his poetic itinerary in *Ragion poetica e programma del verso libero* (1908; "Poetic Rationale and a Plan for Free Verse"), which he dedicated to the futurist Marinetti. Often described as a symbolist, Lucini defied traditional metrics. His free-verse poems were inspired by his anarchist sensibilities. They often criticized the church, the state, militarism, and colonialism.

La canzone del giovane eroe

Canzone, soffèrmati,

accogli la voce

gioconda e marziale

del giovane Eroe,

agnello mansueto per le sale,

e, nella mischia, intrepido e feroce.

«—Signore, sono l'Eroe autentico,

quello vivo, splendente nell'assisa,

alle cui braccia la Patria si affida,

sicuramente,

come la vostra noia si confida

al soffice riposo della poltrona.

Signore,

sono l'Eroe;

quando le sorchie vanno in amore,

inforco il destriero, risuono

di sproni, di sciabola e d'albagia.

Venni d'Africa orrenda e tenebrosa,

gesta racconto omeriche:

passione italiana Orlando e Ruggero incitare

nell'eroicomico poema militare.

E vengo dalla China:

per sé stessa indovina, Madame Chrysanthème

seppe far casa polita, però...

The Song of the Young Hero

Song, take a pause:
hear the joyous and martial words
of the young Hero, a mild lamb in the parlors
but fearless lion in a brawl.

Ladies, I'm the true Hero, in the flesh,
shiny in his uniform, in whose arms our Land's
entrusted safely, as your boredom surrenders
to a chaise longue's smooth rest.

Ladies, I am the Hero.
When pussies are in heat,
I vault on my charger, I jingle
my haughty airs, my sword and my spurs.

I came back from dark, ominous Africa[1]
to sing Homer-like feats: it's so Italian
to goad Orlando and Roger[2] on
in mock-heroic poems of war.

I come from China, too; there, clairvoyant
Madame Chrysanthème knew
how to make a clean sweep;[3] unhappily,

---

[1] An allusion to Italy's colonial wars in Eritrea and Abyssinia

[2] Orlando and Ruggero are heroes in Italian epic poems.

[3] Madame Chrysanthème is the heroine of a well-known novel by Pierre Loti (1850–1923).

i sopracciò della diplomazia

mandaron navi, cannoni ed armati,

presti Modugni internazionali

e prestatissimi generali.

Fui là giù e son qui,

Palo di ferro, per servirvi al punto.

Se ho fatto la sciocchezza d'ammogliarmi prima,

con qualche insipida e provinciale ragazzina,

un suicidio provvidenziale, mi diè la spesa del funerale,

ma mi fè libero di convolare a nozze più decenti.

Eccomi, dunque. In previsione,

vi ho recato bottino, Signore, pesante,

perché disprezzo un poco la professione

dello straccione Cavalier errante.

Riportai intatta la virilità,

l'ho riserbata a voi ed alla Patria:

posso offrirvi per dono

babbuccie ricamate, aspre di perle,

grandi vasi di *vecchio Giappone*,

in torno a cui s'avvoltola un dragone,

le fauci spalancate e l'ali aperte,

the know-it-alls of diplomacy
sent ships, soldiers, and guns,[4]
sly cosmopolitan Modugni[5]
and mercenary generals.

I was there and am here,
Mr. Erect, to serve you to a tee.
If I was fool enough to get hitched up
to an insipid, small-town gal,
a providential suicide made me shell
out for the funeral, but let me
march down the aisle to a better match.
So here I am. Anticipating,
I brought some weighty booty, Ladies,
for I look down at the profession
of a Knight-Errant dressed in rags.

I brought back my virility, too,
preserved for Motherland and you,
and can offer as gifts embroidered slippers
seeded with pearls, and vases
of old Japan with coiled dragons on them,
bared fangs and wings outspread,

---

[4] An allusion to a body of Italian soldiers sent to China during the Boxer Rebellion in 1900

[5] Modugno was a lieutenant who took part in the expedition to China and became notorious for his brutality and looting.

lacche e avorii scolpiti,

un piccolo *bazar di chinoiseries*

tutto per voi e... il resto oh,... *m'amies!*

Perciò desidero d'andare a Tripoli,

pacifico guerriero,

per procacciarvi stoffe, arazzi, cuscini,

nielli damaschini, artifizii novelli ed orientali

d'aggiungere in collana ai vizii europei delle guarnigioni,

per ritentar, con voi, sopra a queste dovizie,

in mille modi e svariato costume,

paradisiache blandizie, quella faccenda,... sì...;

lasciate dire;... non arrossite così.

Per le Dame che fanno le preziose

ho drappi del colore d'amaranto;

per le troppo pudiche

lunghi veli di seta sul talamo;

per le sfacciate, ecco larghe conchiglie di sete rosate

a paragone delle membra nude,

pallide, ambrate, vive giunchiglie:

per tutte, fiori a profusione,

profumi, carezze, sollazzo.

Ho un gran palazzo in fantasia,

e molta cortesia.

lacquerware and carved ivory,

a little arsenal of chinoiseries

that's all for you, and the rest . . . oh! . . . *m'amies!*

Therefore I want to go

to Tripoli as a peace-loving warrior,

to get you bolts of cloth, tapestries, pillows,

and damascened scrimshaw,

and new oriental artifacts

to add to the collections

of our kinky garrisons,

to try again with you, on top of these goodies,

in a thousand ways and in disparate fashions,

heavenly endearments . . . in a few words . . . the act:

yes, let me say it. Please, do not blush like that.

For ladies hard to please I have

amarinthine brocades;

for the excessively shy

chiffon veils on the bed;

and for the saucy, conch shells full

of silks as rosy as naked limbs:

·pale, amber, lively jonquils;

for each and every one, a bounty of flowers,

hugs, perfume, merrymaking.

In my imagination I possess

a sumptuous palace

and excellent finesse.

Signore,

sono l'irresistibile;

alla punta de' baffi si aduna,

col fluido d'eleganza, il magnetismo e l'attrazione

per la maschia prestanza.

Le mie pupille ladre

brillano come spalline d'argento,

donde schiumeggian le spesse ciniglie

in sulle spalle quadre d'Ercole adolescente,

e fan da ruba cuori.

Sono l'irresistibile;

passai tra le battaglie indisturbato,

sorridendo e giuocando col mughetto,

che la bella mi aveva donato,

arcangiolo corrusco e impomatato,

nobile Alfiere de' Lancieri del Re.

Badate a me:

posso offrirvi una notte di amore?

L'ozio m'irrita della caserma,

la cavalcata mattutina mi eccita,

il fruscio delle gonne mi snerva;

amare, Signore, è necessario,

come combattere, come... conquistare

colonie alla Patria, che attende e conserva,

sul libro della storia, la nostra gloria.

Ladies, I'm irresistible;

on the tips of my mustache gather,

with elegance incarnate,

the charm and magnetism

of my masculine beauty.

Stealing your hearts,

my roguish pupils dart

like my silver epaulets

whence foam the broad ribbons and chevrons

on the square shoulders of adolescent Hercules.

I'm irresistible;

unscathed, I went through battles

smiling and sporting a lily of the valley

that my sweet gave me—

glowing, pomaded angel, noble ensign

of the King's lancers.

What do you say: may I

offer you a night of love?

The barracks' inaction irks me,

my early rides excite me,

rustling skirts enervate me.

Ladies, love's a necessity,

like fighting, like . . . conquering colonies

for the Motherland that waits for

and keeps, in history's book, our glory.

Oggi, le nubi vanno e poi ritornano

varie d'umore e di colori,

fumo leggiero e inconsistente, fumo di Parlamento.

Sul sì e sul no ambigui,

credete a me, amiamoci con squisita innocenza.

Ecco, Signore, in molta confidenza,

dentro al cerchio sottile dell'orecchio,

padiglione di morbidi secreti

seminascosto dai biondi riccioli,

posso io confidare parole, consigli e voluttà?...

Non arrossite, Signore, non iscordo

l'obbligo mio di nobiltà.

Camere ammobigliate

e cene in *cabinet particulier*,

per le borghesi; vino d'Asti e *sandwichs*

ripieni di prosciutto e di caviale,

ostriche di Taranto per le ballerine;

tartufi a volontà.

E poi, che fa?

Venni d'Africa orrenda e tenebrosa,

e venni dalla China;

mi sono conservato,

ho provveduto, eroicamente,

al mio a venire e alla magnificenza della Nazione,

per nostra mutua soddisfazione.

Today the clouds come and go,

varied in mood and hue,

like evanescent smoke, smoke of our Parliament.

Ambiguous about yes and no, please listen:

let's love each other with untainted innocence.

So, Ladies, in full confidence,

inside the delicate shell of your ear,

pavillion of soft secrets

half hidden by blond hair,

may I pour words of advice and delight?

Ladies, don't blush: I'm not so crass

as to ignore the duties of my class.

Furnished rooms and dinners for two

for bourgeois dames; caviar

and ham canapés, Asti wine

and Taranto oysters for escorts.

Plenty of truffles, too.

And next, what will he do?

I came back from dark, ominous Africa,[6]

and China, too.

I've stayed alive

to heroically provide

for my future and the greatness of our Nation,

to the gratification of us both.

---

[6] Lucini was the first Italian poet to make fun of Mussolini's African wars.

Signore,

tra le quattro e le sei, nell'ora psicologica,

posso offrirvi un rinfresco d'amore?—»

Canzone, confessa che alla guerra,

si mangia bene e non si dorme per terra.

Ladies, between four and six,

the perfect time to mix, may I

fix you a love cocktail?

Song, admit it: in times of war

one eats well and sleeps not on the floor.

La canzone della cortigianetta

Canzone, se ti attardi

nei Caffé di mezza notte,

quando corruscano di lacche e di specchi,

d'argenterie, di marmi e porcellane,

ai mille becchi de' candelabri di cristallo e d'oro,

e sciaman le ragazze in *décolletées*,

di *souteneurs* e di gaudenti;

Canzone, ascolta,

tra la fucileria del bacchico *champagne*,

canto giocondo ed arrochito:

raccogline le note, conservane i versi,

dedicalo lezione alle adolescenti

della fervida e nobile Città.

Canzone; questa è stramba parata urbana,

che sgola una Fata discinta ed ebra un poco:

discese, Cenerentola, un giorno da una fiaba estemporanea

tra i gatti e i passeri della grondaja,

per infilar la seta nella cruna astrusa,

e puntar l'ago contro il ditale,

e il filo dentro ad un raso nuziale:

Canzone, lascia cantar la Fata

con un nodo di pianto alla strozza,

col riso che singhiozza tra le lagrime.

The Song of the Young Courtesan

Song, if you linger in midnight cabarets

when they shimmer

with lacquer, silver, and mirrors,

marble and china, by the thousand prisms

of gold and crystal chandeliers,

and girls in décolleté

swarm among pimps and revelers,

listen, song, through the artillery

of the Bacchic champagne,

to a joyful and harsh tune:

gather its notes, keep its lines, dedicate it—

a lesson—to young girls

of the busy, grand City.[1]

Song: here's an odd city exhibition hawked

by a flimsily dressed Fairy, slightly drunk.

One day she came out, Cinderella, of an improvised fable

among the cats and sparrows in the eaves

to put the silk through the difficult eye

of the needle and press

against thimble and thread

inside a nuptial satin.

Song, let the Fairy sing

with a lump in her throat

and laughter mixed with tears.

---

[1] The city is Milan.

«—Per la più facile felicità

sono, fra voi, autoctona regina della moda,

per l'ambizione del giovane banchiere,

e l'arroganza del biscazziere.

Oggi, ho imparato, in breve scuola,

ad offrirmi, a fuggire, a tentennare,

a bilanciarmi in sull'ambiguo giuoco della parola.

Qualche volta mi pesa la bugia;

mi dolgo; è lievito del tempo antico ed abolito,

che fermenta e pretende intumidirsi,

rammarico, ricordo, inattuale pretesto a piangere.

Davanzale del piccolo abbaino,

sporto sul tetto a cappuccina,

primo ad accoglier il sole a mattina,

erto sopra le tegole a guardar l'oriente intenerito;

pensile giardinetto di quattro vasetti

dove sfiammavano insanguinando il verde

garofani plebei, garibaldini spavaldi e procaci;

minuscolo divano dove imparai

le prime lagrime e i primi baci,

e sopportai le prime prurigini moleste;

cameretta inondata di luce,

dove in un vortice brunito d'acciaio,

battevano al volante l'agili membra della silente macchina,

svolgendo il filo del mobile rocchetto

"For the most simple happiness, I am—

among you—self-sufficient fashion queen,

to satisfy the young banker's ambition

and the arrogance of gamblers.

Today, schooled quickly, I've learned

to give myself, to flee, to hesitate,

to walk a tightrope on ambiguous plays on words.

At times, lying annoys me; I feel sorry.

It's yeast of old, abolished days

that ferments and expects to swell again—

regret, remembrance, dumb pretext for crying.

Cute attic windowsill

that jutted out over the petaled tiles,

the first to welcome sun rays in the morning,

oustretching to look tenderly at the East;

hanging garden of four pots where

poor carnations flamed forth, bloodying the green

like Garibaldi's sexy, boasting army;[2]

minuscule sofa where I knew

the first tears and first kisses

and put up with the first pesty itches;

little room flooded with light

where in a whirl burnished with steel

the mute machine's sprite limbs marched to the wheel's

---

[2] Garibaldi's soldiers wore red shirts.

e regolando l'impuntura all'ago,

dentro alle stoffe, isocrona e perfetta;

o cameretta, dove a me piacque

numerare sul ritmo dell'ordigno,

il battere nell'arterie, dal polso al cuore,

del mio giovane sangue caldo ed eletto:

colazioni frugali, sperso l'occhio al frullar breve dell'ali

dei passeri sul tetto, al dondolar del ceppo di garofano,

sui lunghi steli; ozio breve, gustato in fretta;

sognar lontano, presto risvegliato;...

antica istoria: tutte le sere udite

Mimí Pinson gorgheggiar *La Bohéme*.

Ma la crisalide si fa vanessa,

farfalla splendida multicolore;

e il bigio bozzolo che l'ha incubata,

in una palazzina delicata.

Eccomi esperta cantarina apocrifa

col pretesto di ricche acconciature,

sopra li avvisi a finger le avventure della ribalta:

ed eccomi a recare cure e pazienza per tutti i gusti

sì che i più frusti vengono a me.

Sono un albergo ad insegna cortese;

se muto stile, cognome e pretese

rinnovo i desideri.

Dovunque mi presento come vuole il costume;

tempo, unwinding the thread of the spool

and gauging, isochronal and perfect,

the needle's stitch onto the wool.[3]

O tiny room, where I loved

to count, to the machine's rhythm,

the beat in my veins, from wrist to heart,

of my young, hot, and selected blood;

frugal breakfasts, my gaze lost in the flutter

of sparrows' wings on the roof, swaying carnation

blooms on their stems; short breaks, enjoyed in haste;

same old story: each night a *chanson*

from *La bohéme* by Pinsòn.[4]

But the chrysalis turns into *Vanessa*,

a gorgeous, multicolored butterfly;

and the beige cocoon that incubated her

into a dainty villa is modified.

So here I am, consummate spurious singer

wrapped in stunning hairdos to carry out

on playbills the adventures of the stage.

Here I am to serve and tolerate all tastes,

so that even the lowest come to me.

I'm a hotel with a friendly sign;

if I change style, last name, and desires,

I spark new fires.

I go everywhere as fashion would have it;

---

[3] The machine is a sewing machine.

[4] Pinsòn is the heroine of a short story by Musset and the main character in Puccini's opera.

tutto quanto posseggo in carne viva

vi offro e vi dò sotto la veste a scialo

e sotto la camicia trasparente,

come un miraggio all'imaginazione

per la lussuria grassa della gente.

Eccovi il volto che il rossetto avviva,

oh! quante volte come triste e smorto:

sbatte il ventaglio ed agita le lunghe piume bianche,

al capo reclinato; cercan riposo e schermo

alla luce, alli sguardi, all'insistenze le mie pupille stanche;

colle palpebre basse, cerco dimenticarmi.

E udite risa che scrosciano a trilli,

gorgoglian soffocate sotto una furia di baci improvvisi,

scendono, mancano dentro la gola,

fremitano nel collo col singhiozzo...

oh! quanta angoscia di risa convulse,

quanto soffrire per la voluttà.

Borghesi, io vi balocco: re di corona, a me:

sovverto l'ordine, la disciplina,

ed il burocrata a me vicino torna bambino.

La mia carne è ingemmata,

le membra ammorbidite e stilizzate

a richiesta dell'epoca:

i petali di rosa son meno teneri e profumati

delle mie coscie;

il mio piedino detta la legge;

whatever living flesh I own

under my petticoat and corset

is all yours to indulge in—

like a mirage is to the imagination—

to satisfy the people's prurient vision.

Here is the face, so often sad and pale,

that the blusher enlivens: the fan twirls

.and waves its long white feathers at the bowed head;

my tired eyes look for shelter and rest

from light, from glances, from requests;

with eyelids shut, I try to block it out.

So you hear laughter cascading in rills,

gurgling smothered by sudden frenzies

of kisses, lowering, fading in the throat,

then rising, quivering, mixed with sobs . . .

oh! so much anguish of frantic laughter,

so much pain for our pleasure.

Bourgeois, I pull the strings, I—queen of hearts:

I subvert order and discipline; the bureaucrat

with me becomes a babe. As to my flesh,

bedecked with jewels, my limbs softened, stylized

as taste dictates—

rose petals are less tender

and perfumed than my thighs;

my dainty foot commands;

l'indice teso segna una vittima;

il monosillabo condanna a morte, se nega e rifiuta.

Cammino e regno:

le scarpine lingueggian dalla gonna,

orme suggellano ne' cuori molli, e nella polvere;

i fianchi ondeggiano al passo ritmico e birichino;

s'inarcano le terga in curva callipigia;

scutrettola la trina dello strascico,

coda occellata d'Imperatrice e di Sirenetta.

Domino; attraggo; respingo e mi prometto:

spargete fiori sul mio passaggio,

nobili e grandi d'ogni lignaggio;

rido, ed ancheggio e sbadiglio:

son la bellissima fatalità.

Sono l'Eterno biondo Feminino;

colle mani propino affusolate,

che il manicure mi ha raccomandate,

filtri che odorano di sortilegio,

carezze irresistibili,

esca, ragna ed agguato prelibato.

Borghesi, io vi balocco;

come un giorno mio padre pitocco,

che, ad ingannar la fame,

my finger names its victims;

my monosyllable, if it says no and thumbs down,

gives a death sentence.

I walk and reign: my little shoes dart out

from underneath my gown, stamping their imprint

on both faint hearts and dust;

my hips sway to a rhythmic, impish step;

my derrière arches in a callipygian curve;

the lace on my train wiggles, spotted tail

of Empress and Mermaid.

I dominate, attract, encourage, boo.

Strew flowers on my path,

grandees and princes from all stations;

I laugh, waddle, and yawn.

I'm fate, in all its charm.

I am the blond She, the Ageless One;[5]

with these exquisite hands

my beautician commends

I sell love potions brewed in sorcery,

unbeatable caresses,

bait, spider's web, and tender trap.

Bourgeois, I pull the strings

as one day my poor father

to kill his hunger juggled

---

[5] A parody of "Ewig-Weibliche" in the penultimate line of Goethe's *Faust,* mediated
by Carducci's "eterno femminino regale"

ballonzolava pietre in sulla strada

dall'una all'altra mano

e le stringeva in pugno,

guardando al di là delle siepi i giardini

colmi di frutti maturi,

e, in sulle panche, sotto le pergole,

soffici cuscini per li ozi sicuri.

Sono l'Eterno biondo Feminino;

per una sessuale complicità

non so tenere il broncio;

sporgo sempre il bocchino:

risuggelliam la pace,

e l'oblío che rinchiude il secreto dell'anima ancora,

che serra, nella carne colla carne, le porte

alla vita impaziente, e lo conserva sino alla morte.

Ma a te solo, che sei là giù in fondo e mi guardi,

coi grandi occhi pensosi e conturbati,

ho riserbata una verginità, Signore, insospettata.

Dirò a te, che comprendi, le nostalgie inutili,

le reticenze, le angoscie, le pazzie,

e desideri vani e le impossibili malinconie.

Ed odimi, Signore, finché mi regge il cuore

dentro a questa tormenta che sembra giorno calmo;

ed odimi, amico di pietà sincera,

nella bufera de' sensi e de' capricci...

assicurarmi la profezia.

slick pebbles in the street

and caught them in his fist,

looking beyond the hedges at the gardens

loaded with luscious fruit

and on the benches, under bowers,

fluffy cushions for untroubled hours of ease.

I am the blond She, the Ageless One.

Since we're partners in sex, I cannot pout

and always give my wanton lips;

then we make peace again, with that forgetfulness

that yet encloses the secret of the soul

and shuts the doors, in the meeting of the flesh,

to impatient life, and keeps it until death.

Only for you, who over there do stare

at me, perturbed and thoughtful,

Sir, I have kept most surprisingly pure.

Since you understand, I'll tell you of vain nostalgia,

reticence, madness, pain,

fruitless pursuits, overwhelming despair.

Please hear me, Sir,

as long as my heart can

face the storm that you see as fair weather;

hear me, you friend who take sincerest pity,

set down my prophecy

smack in the whorl of whims and senses.

Fra poco scenderò larva crepuscolare,

se il sol di mezza notte contrafatto non mi giova più,

sciupata rondinella delle strade.

Sarò il rifiuto della grande Città:

quando piove ed abbrivida la sera,

quando le gocciole, sotto ai riverberi,

sembrano spine d'argento a pungere

contro il fango, la carne ed il cuore;

sarò l'ombra vagante e pandemia,

che scivola con passo pornografico,

per le viuzze e i trivi tentando *pis, pis,*

come un richiamo e come una preghiera.

Sarò, sotto ai fanali de' passeggi pubblici,

al primo che mi accolga e non s'accorga

del mio volto disfatto, dell'abiti stinti;

sarò all'affamato per lungo digiuno

per chi paga, t'insozza e ti disprezza.

Sarò l'illusione dell'amore,

per rinnovare, offertorio di grazia,

la mia sapienza ringiovanita,

all'imberbe che spasima e si disseta,

febrile, spaventato, come a una prima notte,

sacerdotessa compresa e insoddisfatta,

vergognosa e crudele maestra di vita.

D'oggi a dimani sarò il vituperio

de' vostri ricchi vizii, decaduta;

In a short while I'll come, an evening ghost,
if the fake midnight sun helps me no more,
bruised swallow in the street.

I'll be the refuse of the famous City,
and when it rains and the evening is trembling,
and raindrops, in the glare,
seem silver thorns that dart
into mud, flesh, the heart,
I'll be a wandering, public shadow,
gliding with pornographic steps
through lanes and crossroads, whispering my offer,
half call half prayer.

Under the park walks' lamplight I shall be
for the first one who takes me and doesn't see
my ravaged face and faded clothes;
I'll serve whoever fasted and now starves;
whoever pays, sullies, and then despises.

I will be love's illusion to confirm
rejuvenated wisdom to the fledgling
that feverishly frets and sates his thirst
as if on the first night, afraid.
I'll be the Priestess—understood, unquenched—
shameful and hard master of life.

Between today and tomorrow I'll be the fallen
reproach of your rich vices, be the one

sarò le vostre passioni, inconfessate;

vi verrò in contro colle mani tese,

non mi vorrete conoscere più.

Vi ricompenserò coll'odio e col veleno,

che distilla il mio sesso e che mi abbrucia;

passerò su di voi, sulla vostra famiglia,

come il castigo, come l'uragano,

larva di disonore e di fanghiglia,

come un'angiola nera di vendicazione.

Ora ridiamo; ho i miei biondi perché

innumerevoli testardi e ricci

e folti e varii e molti come i ricci

de' miei capelli foggiati in topé.

Tu, Signore, pensoso e conturbato

fammi portar da bere acqua ghiacciata.

Non ci badare, tutto è passato; sono momenti di debolezza,

vengono e vanno colla tristezza

e il lungo brivido di mezza notte.

L'estetica ironia stelleggia il cielo

oscuro, in curva sui campanili;

nei cuori pigri e spenti suscita incanti

sciupa parole alate

sopra il belletto delle labra esangui—.»

Canzon bella e sfacciata, con fervore,

se ti piace, di' pur: «*Qui regna amore.*»

with your unavowed quirks.

I'll come to you with open arms;

you will pretend not to have known me, ever.

And I'll repay you with the hate and poison

my sex distills, making me burn:

I'll come upon you and your family

like doom, like a tornado,

larva of infamy and mud,

black angel of revenge.

But now let's laugh. I have my blond *raisons*:

countless, stubborn, and frizzy

like my curls shaped into a *chignon*.

Yes, Sir, upset and pensive:

have some iced water brought me, if you please.

Don't mind me, all is forgotten; these are moments

of weakness coming and going with sadness

and the protracted shiver of midnight.

Aesthetic irony stars the dark sky

spilling over the steeples;

in lazy and flameless hearts it kindles charms,

wastes wingèd words

on the gloss of white lips . . ."

Stunning, impudent song, if you like, say

with ardor: *"This is where Love holds sway."*[6]

---

[6] An ironic quotation from Petrarch (*De remediis utriusque fortunae* 126.52)

Between Art Deco and the Twilight Poets

CORRADO GOVONI

Corrado Govoni was born in Tamaro, near Ferrara, in 1884 into a family of well-off farmers. He self-published his first collections of poetry, *Le fiale* ("Vials") and *Armonia in grigio et in silenzio* ("Harmony in Gray and in Silence"), in 1903. He subsequently published various collections of poetry—such as *Gli aborti* (1907; "Abortions") and *Rarefazioni e parole in libertà* (1915; "Rarefactions and Words in Freedom")—plays, novels, and short stories and contributed to many literary journals (including *La voce* ["The Voice"] and *Lacerba*), all the while supporting himself through a variety of odd jobs. In 1944 Govoni's son Aladino was killed by Nazis at the infamous massacre at the Ardeatine caves. Govoni died at Lido dei Pini, near Rome, in 1965. With Corazzini, he is considered one of the first crepuscular or twilight poets. Accordingly, the natural world has a strong presence in his work, and in many of his poems simple objects (shrubs, trumpets, statues) come to life. Govoni's oeuvre, however, is quite varied, and it is difficult to place him in a specific movement; he has been called hermetic, crepuscular, and futurist, to give a few labels.

Cavallo

Violenta primavera del cavallo!
Ad ogni suo elastico passo
intorno allo zoccolo viola
che stampa lune di rumore, fuma
un biancospino di polvere,
sboccia un cespuglio di fango.

Siepe

All'odore crudele
che viene dalle spine della siepe
il tuo sangue amareggia l'amore,
e ti diventan gli occhi
una luce cattiva pigiata.
Sulla tua statua che cammina
aprendo una nuova strada nel vento
invano battono le mie parole
come gocce di rugiada da me scossa.
Prego l'erba dell'argine ti venga incontro
con la lampada avvelenata del gigaro
per far soffrire la tua bocca rossa.

Horse

Wild springtime of the horse!
At each elastic step of his
on purple hooves that imprint moons of noise
a dusty hawthorn smokes, a mud bush blooms.

Hedge

As the pitiless scent
comes from the hedge's thorns,
your blood embitters love, your eyes become
a mean, squashed light.
Like dewdrops I shake off,
uselessly my words fight you—
a statue cutting a new path in the wind.
I hope the grass on the bank turns
toward you with the torch of poison ivy
to make your red mouth burn.

Il palazzo dell'anima

Triste dimora! Aborti nelle fiale,

rachitici e verdastri. Sorridenti

bambole sparse ovunque. Sofferenti

in vasi d'ambra fior di digitale.

Campane di cristallo su agonie

di cera, rosee maschere di seta

annegate nell'acqua ovale inquieta

degli specchi, malinconie impagliate.

Laggiù la città bianca col suo rombo

d'api e il suo fiume di ardente piombo,

come un pallido sogno di morfina.

Oh i crepuscoli tristi d'anilina

sulle mura echeggianti di fanfare!

Da una finestra si scorge il mare.

Palace of the Soul

Sad dwellings! Fetuses in tubes,
greenish and stunted. Strewn
everywhere, smiling dolls. Aswoon
in amber vases, flowers of foxgloves.

Silver bells on wax agonies,
pink masks of silk
drowned in the restless oval water
of mirrors, stuffed despondencies.

In the distance the city with its river
of molten lead and its droning of bees—
morphia's own pallid reveries.

Sad, ethylene twilight
on walls resounding with fanfares!
From a window the ocean is in sight.

ALDO PALAZZESCHI

Aldo Palazzeschi was born as Aldo Giurlani in Florence in 1885, into a bourgeois family. He was educated in accounting but spent his earlier years acting; then he dedicated himself to writing. Although Palazzeschi began his literary career as a poet—collections include *L'incendiario* (1910; "The Incendiary"; dedicated to Marinetti) and *Poesie* (1930; "Poems")—he is best known for his novel *Le sorelle Materassi* (1934; "The Materassi Sisters"). He continued to publish manifestos, poetry, and novels until his death in Rome in 1974. Like Govoni, he is hard to classify. While his earlier poems share affinities with the crepuscular poets, he also wrote futurist and surrealist verse. In his provocative, humorous, and grotesque poems he frequently employs irony, satire, and comedy to criticize social convention or highlight nihilism.

Il ritratto di Corinna Spiga

Vorresti, Peonia, cavar la tovaglia?
La cena è finita oramai,
quel bianco stasera m'abbaglia,
non sembra un lenzuolo?

Rimetti, rimetti il tappeto,
fai presto, mia buona Peonia,
non posso guardare quel legno,
ha un brutto colore, nevvero?

Vorresti, Giuditta,
provare ad alzare quel lume,
mi sembra sia gialla la luce, ti pare?
È vero, mia piccola?
Così, Giulietta, così.

Tu tieni, Celeste,
le mani così sulla tavola insieme,
mi sembran di cera...
mi sembran le dita sì lunghe...

Bianca, tu tieni
la testa poggiata, perché?
Vedessi l'effetto che fa...
sei bianca,

Corinna Spiga's Portrait

Peony, would you mind
putting the tablecloth away?
Dinner is over now. Today
that white's making me blind.

Unroll the rug once more,
my good Peony, do it;
I can't stand the bare floor,
it's a nasty color, ain't it?

Ah, Judith, will you try
to raise the wick?
the light's yellow and sick;
please do comply.

Celeste, you hold your hands
so close together on the table,
they look like marble to me,
the fingers point like wands . . .

Bianca, your head is hung
low. Why? You should see
what you look like . . . you're white,

e paiono gli occhi

socchiusi a metà.

Sei stanca mia piccola, forse?

Mia cara Fanny,

sei muta anche tu.

Le tue labbra

non hanno un sorriso più.

Oh! la tua bocca serrata, Fanny,

che pena! che pena!

Ti par di sentire...

rumore giù all'uscio?

Non è vero, Maddalena?

Rumore di passi, strisciare...

posare qualcosa...

Che è mai, chi mormora giù,

che voci, che luci son quelle,

chi batte, chi entra?

Correte, chiudetegli in faccia le porte,

venite, venite, venite mie figlie,

mie povere figlie,

stringetemi, stringetemi forte:

Corinna! Corinna! Corinna!

and your eyes seem half closed.

My little one, are you

tired, maybe?

My dear Fanny,

you're quiet, too.

Your lips no longer smile.

Ah! your tight mouth, Fanny,

How pitiful it is!

Don't you think you just heard

some noise down at the door?

Magdalene, is it so?

Sounds of steps, something shuffling . . .

stopping . . . Who can it be,

who's whispering down there,

what voices, lights are those,

who's knocking, coming in?

Run, shut the door in his face,

come, come, my daughters, race,

hold me to your last breath:

It's death! It's death! It's death![1]

---

[1] I translate freely, choosing a rhyme instead of the literal "Corinna! Corinna! Corinna!"

Visita alla Contessa Eva Pizzardini Ba

—Buonasera contessa.

—Buonasera, carissimo Aldo.

—Oggi giornata bella, contessa.

—Troppo bella, carissimo Aldo,

non fa né freddo... né caldo.

—E... la noia, contessa?

—La che?...

—La no-ia.

—Pa... pa... papa... papa.

—Sempre la stessa.

—Ciò mi dite di nuovo?

Bravo.

—Cosa dirvi di nuovo?

Mi credete così ingenuo?

Nemmeno mi ci provo.

—Bravo.

E passate per giovine bizzarro...

per uomo... tanto strano.

Strano... bizzarro...

bizzarro... strano...

Bravo.

—Codesta bella veste, contessa,

la vidi proprio iersera

precisa... a una borghese.

—E fu inventata a Parigi

A Visit to the Countess Eva Pizzardini Ba

—Good evening, countess.

—Good evening, my dear Aldo.

—And what a lovely day.

—Too lovely, darling:

neither cold nor stifling.

—And your boredom, countess?

—My what?

—Boredom.

—It's martyrdom.

—Always the same.

—Is that what's new?

Ooh.

—What news should I have? Why?

You think me so naive?

I will not even try.

—Oh my.

And they think you're such a droll young fry . . .

such a . . . weird, weird man.

Odd . . . droll . . .

Droll . . . odd . . .

Good.

—Your beautiful dress, countess.

I saw it just last night

on a . . . bourgeois. The same.

—And it was made in Paris

che non è ancora un mese:

sempre così, si sa.

—A Parigi fumano l'oppio.

—A Parigi...

—Verrà presto la moda anche da noi.

—Certo verrà, poi.

Le belle cose da noi sono un mito,

noi siamo quelli di ieri... o di poi.

Che governo pitocco!

Ma... di nuovo?

—Di nuovo...

la gallina ha fatto l'uovo.

—Ecco.

Bella consolazione,

dover vivere tanto

per veder tutti i giorni

le medesime cose.

Giunge il sole e se ne va,

cresce e cala la luna.

Sempre uguale il sole,

la luna è sempre uguale,

non cambian di colore.

Identiche le stelle.

—Purtroppo.

—Azzurro il cielo

azzurro il mare:

val la pena

hardly a month ago:

always like this, you know.

—In Paris, they smoke opium.

—Yes, à Paree . . .

—The trend will soon be here.

—Of course it will. But later.

Grand things stay mythical with us;

we go with yesterday . . . or the future.

Our government: phew!

But . . . what's new?

—New . . . a hen

has laid an egg.

—Dregs.

What wretched consolation

to have to live so long

just to see every day

the selfsame throng.

The sun comes, the sun goes,

the moon waxes and wanes.

Sun and moon never alter

and the stars never falter.

—Ooh.

—The sky is blue

and blue too the sea:

why open the window,

di aprire una finestra per guardare?

—Ma...

—Verde il prato

verde il bosco:

il color vostro lo conosco, ahimé.

—Non ci badate.

—Si aspettano le solite persone

alle solite ore,

che ci vengon davanti

con la solita faccia,

non è facile sbagliare,

e con identica voce

ci dicono le identiche parole.

E non giova il cambiare,

che se pure ti sembrano

l'uno all'altro diversi

nelle forme o gli aspetti,

ti diran tutti alla stessa maniera:

«Buongiorno contessa,

contessa, buonasera.»

Tutti i giorni si nasce...

e tutti i giorni si muore.

Quando si nasce c'è la levatrice,

quando si muore... c'è il dottore.

—Preferisco la levatrice.

—Io no, il dottore.

Che ci si viene a fare?

what's new there to see?

—But . . .

—Green is the meadow,

the wood is green;

and I know what your color has been.

—Don't let it be a burden.

—We wait for the same persons

at the expected time and place,

they come to greet us

with the same old face,

it's not easy to miss,

and with the same whine

they recite the same line.

Change is useless, you see,

for even seeming different

to you to some degree

in their shapes or their looks,

they'll tell you the same way:

"Good night, dear countess;

countess, good day."

Every day one is born . . .

every day one leaves life.

When you're born there's a midwife.

A doctor when you die.

—I prefer the midwife.

—Oh no. The doctor, I.

What do we come here for?

Che si fa?

Si può sapere?

Si sa?

—Calmatevi, contessa.

—E dire che vorrei, solo per una volta,

vedermi nuova nel mio specchio.

—Come?

—Nuova, diversa da sempre,

e diversa da tutte.

—Aver due bocche?

—Magari, ma è un caso comune.

—Lo so. Un occhio dietro?

—Dove?

—Nella testa.

—Ah, sì...

—Un dente sulla punta del naso?

—Meglio senza naso, nel caso.

—Due teste?

—Comune comune.

—Sette teste? Tredici gambe?

—Comune comune.

Ieri sera per dormire

mi son fatta tre volte

la puntura di morfina.

—Tre volte!

—Sono poche? Sono molte?

—Ma vi pare? La morfina!

And what to do?

Can we ever know?

Is there anyone who?

—Calm down, countess.

—Think I would like, for once,

to see myself

new at the looking glass.

—How, new?

—Unique, not usual,

and forever apart from any lass.

—To have two mouths?

—Maybe, but that's so trite.

—Quite. An eye in the back?

—Where?

—Of your head.

—Oh, yeah . . .

—On your nosetip a tooth?

—Better no nose, in truth.

—Two heads?

—Horribly plain.

—Seven heads? Thirteen feet?

—The pits.

Last night to sleep

I had myself injected

three times with morphine.

—Three times? *Parbleu!*

—Why, too many? Too few?

—What do you mean, morphine?

—«La morfina!» La mor-fi-na.

—Vorreste diventare d'un tratto

regina o imperatrice?

Antonietta? Messalina!

—Uhm... forse sarebbe meglio...

—Una poveretta.

—Forse.

—Povera molto, vivere d'elemosina,

essere giù, nel fango...

—Forse.

—Insultata...

—Certo.

—Battuta...

—Almeno.

—Magari nel mezzo della strada

sull'ultimo gradino dell'abiezione,

come una donna perduta.

—Sì.

—Venduta.

—Sì.

—Essere vilipesa... prostituta!

—Insultata... battuta... venduta...

almeno per provare,

ma... come fare, noi...

Chi ci può insultare?

—Voi? Io.

—Morphine, I say: as set.

—Would you change on a bet

into an empress or a queen?

Antoinette? Messalina!

—Perhaps it would be better . . .

—A poor woman. I know.

—Maybe so.

—To live off alms, in misery,

to be down, in the mire . . .

—How dire.

—Abused . . .

—For sure.

—Beaten . . .

—At least.

—Perhaps right in the street,

down to the lowest step

of degradation, like a woman lost.

—At any cost.

—Sold.

—Veritable gold.

—To be insulted . . . prostituted! . . .

—Insulted, beaten, sold . . .

we should give it a try,

but how to do it, you and I?

Who can insult us?

—You? I.

—Siete troppo gentile, poveretto.

—Eccomi qua.

—Siete troppo corretto.

—Mi proverò.

—E non riuscirete

che a noiarmi di più.

—Ma... proviamo.

—E ci tenete tanto?

—Oh! Dio... così... tanto per fare.

—Dirò io per la prima.

—Sentiamo.

—Ma no, ma via, ma no,

perché?... no... povero sciocco, no...

—Stupida d'una donna.

—... poetucolo... pitocco.

—Vescica con la gonna.

—Imbecille! Cretino!

Omo... da nulla.

—Povera grulla!

—Grullone! Scimunito!

Rammollito! Buffone!

—Smencitissima vacca!

Porcona, puttana, vigliacca!...

—Basta basta basta,

mio carissimo Aldo,

non crediamo di dirci

qualche cosa di nuovo,

—You're too kind, my weak man.

—Yet here I am.

—You're too correct.

—Yet let me have a go.

—You'll succeed only

in boring me even more.

—Well . . . I still want.

—You care so much?

—Oh my! Just for the sake of it.

—I'll be the first to go.

—Be it so.

—I can't, I won't, why? Oh!

No, silly one, no . . . no.

—You female with no brain.

—Miser . . . Scribbler in vain.

—Tube with a skirt on.

—Imbecile! Moron!

—Good for nothing . . . sot.

—Little idiot!

—Big idiot! Stubborn mule!

You spineless fool!

—Sagging whore! Yellow belly,

sow, festering sore!

—No more, no more, no more,

Aldo, my dear,

let's not kid ourselves,

there is nothing new here.

sensazione nuova io già non provo,

la cerco, ma non la trovo.

Amiamoci piuttosto,

l'amore è tanto vecchio...

mi sembrerà più nuovo.

— Sì? Purché voi ritorniate come allora.

— Quando?

— Quando mi ascoltavate

senza pensare al male,

ed erano assai meno tediose

le vostre serate.

— Mi avete amata voi?

Ed io vi ho amato, ohibò!

— Non dico questo, no...

— Doveva essere molto noioso

il nostro povero amore

se lo abbiamo troncato

e neppure ce ne ricordiamo.

— Era... una parola sola, allora...

Ricordate ieri sera?

— Ieri sera?

— Quella mia parola...

— Quale? Dite, mi fate venir male.

— Quando fu?...

— Certamente vi sbagliate,

fu la sera avanti.

I feel nothing so rare,

I search but it's not there.

Let's love each other, rather.

Love is so old . . .

to me it will seem newer.

—Oh yeah? So long as you

return to what you were.

—When?

—When you listened to me

without thinking of the bad,

and your evenings were

much less tedious and sad.

—Did you ever love me?

I did love you!

—I'm not saying it's not true . . .

—Our love must have

been very disappointing

if we truncated it

and don't even recall it.

—It was one word only, at that time . . .

You remember last night?

—Last night?

—That word of mine . . .

—Which one? Tell me. You make me feel sick.

—When I said it?

—You're mistaken for sure—

'twas the night before last.

—Ve l'avevo già detta?

—Uh! Centomila sere,

capirete, se è sempre la stessa...

Basta, basta, non la ridite,

lasciatemi morire in pace...

sono malata.

—Che sarà di voi?

—Di me?

—Buonanotte contessa.

—Buonanotte, carissimo Aldo.

—Had I said it before?

—Just a thousand times more;

after all, it's always the same . . .

Enough, enough of this game.

Don't say it. Let me die in peace.

I am getting the blues.

—What will become of you?

—Yes. What?

—Countess, good night.

—Good night, dear Aldo. Toodleloo.

Rue de Buci

Caduto in un ignoto

punto di questa terra

e pervaso

dal più dolce smarrimento

ho perduto il senso di me stesso

la provenienza

la direzione

l'orientamento:

La belle fermière

brasserie idéale

gibiers sardines

filets de maquereau

alimentation générale.

Il mio stato è così dolce

e inaspettato

che non mi debbo domandare

donde venni e perché vado

se mi chiedeste a bruciapelo:

«dove

hai succhiato

il latte di una donna?»

rimarrei senza fiato

non avendo più alcun senso

per me

né la parola andata né ritorno

Rue de Buci

Dropped in a strange
part of this world
and all deranged
by the nuttiest confusion
I've lost completely
every sense of myself
start bearings and direction:
La belle fermière

brasserie idéale

gibiers sardines

filets de maquereau

alimentation générale.

My state of mind's
so cool and unexpected
that I don't have
to wonder where I came from
and why I'm going
if you point-blank demanded
"where were you nursed
on mother's milk?"
I would be dazed
since to stay or to go
is a meaningless phrase

Rue de Buci is a renowned street in Paris.

e distinguendo

nella vaghezza di una nebbia

le cose intorno:

Poissonnerie saucisses

Boucherie

graisse de volaille

prix avantageux

location d'habits.

Né passato né futuro

liberato

dalle catene del tempo

quasi volando

più non avverto

il piede sul selciato:

Beaujolais

les bon vins de la vieille garde

Bar

Cave du marché Buci.

E il presente

sconosciuto

in un istante di abbandono

e d'oblio

fa tacere nel mio corpo

in questo punto

la diabolica parola «io»

come in quello di un defunto:

Sensationnelle!

and I make out

objects around

as in a shapeless fog

Poissonerie saucisses

Boucherie

graisse de volaille

prix avantageux

location d'habits.

Neither future nor past

the chains of time unlocked

and nearly flying

I feel no more

my feet on the sidewalk:

Beaujolais

le bons vins de la vieille garde

Bar

Cave du marché Buci.

And the unknown present

in a moment

of rest and ecstasy

silences in my body

as in a dead man's now

the diabolical word "me":

Sensationelle!

Nouvelles peleuses

et nouvelles grattées

Bigarreux du Gard

pois sucrés

endives et navets.

Anche l'errore

con l'estinzione dell'io

venne fugato non visto:

come posso sbagliare

dal momento che più non esisto?

Buci beauté maison sévère

Jeannette

Graineterie Saint-Germain

Eau de table Sainte-Geneviève.

Nulla voglio e nulla so

né desidero più nulla

causa e principio

d'ogni malattia

come dall'aldilà

scorgo solo delle immagini

dei colori in questa nebbia

e una folla sconosciuta

che cerca avidamente

qualche cosa in questa via:

Laitues jardinières

carottes de Créances

Nouvelles peleuses

et nouvelle grattées

Bigarreux du Gard

pois sucrés

endives et navets.

Even mistakes

now that the ego's been evicted

were thrown out undetected:

how can I errors list

since I no longer exist?

Buci beauté maison sévère

Jeannette

Graineterie Saint-Germain

Eau de table Sainte-Geneviève.

Nothing I know

after nothing I go

no desire to gain

cause and beginning

of all pain

as if from the beyond

I only descry images

and colors in this fog

and a mob alien to me

eagerly looking

for something on this street:

Laitues jardinières

carottes de Créances

poireaux de Montlhéry

La vieille France

champignons de Paris.

Perché sapere

perché volere

quando vivere in questa nebbia

è un così sano piacere?

Aux deux nègres

chambre au mois

et à la journée

grande renommée de tripes

à la mode de Caen.

Tanto vaga è la memoria

che vi ha perduto

ogni suo triste rilievo

il peccato

tutto mi sembra bello

tutto mi sembra puro

come nel giorno che sono nato.

O come vivere in terra

l'esistenza di un trapassato:

Boutons jours plissés

Primeurs épicerie

Vapeur bains douches

Au déballage du marché

Crème d'Isigny.

E quel grido tremendo

poireaux de Montlhéry

La vieille France

champignons de Paris.

Why should one know

why should one wish

since living in this fog

gives such untainted bliss?

Aux deux nègres

chambre au mois

et à la journée

grande renommée de tripes

à la mode de Caen.

Memory is

so faint that sin's

been blotted out

with all its sad imprints

all things look pure to me

everything bright

as on the day when I first saw the light.

Or rather, as if on earth

I existed as a sprite:

Boutons jours plissés

Primeurs épicerie

Vapeur bains douches

Au déballage du marché

Crème d'Isigny.

And that tremendous cry

che ti sembra venire

ora dal Paradiso

e ora dall'Inferno

fatto tacere anch'esso

nel modo più deciso

in fondo del mio interno:

Cave de Languedoc

Charcuterie

Tabac

Billard

La bonne viande de Buci.

Ma giunto al limitare

di questa via

come a varco oltremondano

sembra che una voce m'insegua

e taluno mi richiami

col cenno della mano:

«facesti qualche cosa?»

cenno non di comando

né di curiosità riposta

e voce immensamente affettuosa

che si espande nell'aria

per giungere al mio senso

come il profumo di una rosa

e a cui aderisco

quasi vedendo in sogno la risposta:

Oranges juteuses

that seems to come to you

one moment from on high

and another from Hell

it too smothered to silence

once and for all

in the well of my soul:

Cave de Languedoc

Charcuterie

Tabac

Billard

La bonne viande de Buci.

But as I come

to the end of this road

—a path to another world?—

a voice seems to pursue me

and someone motions me

with a wave of his hand:

"did you do anything?"

a voice not of command

or of inner curiosity

a voice so deeply affectionate

that spreads out in the air

to reach my senses

like the scent of a rose

to which I cling

seeing the answer in a dream:

Oranges juteuses

abricots fondants

les bonnes fraises de Lion

poires au couteau

Pierrot gourmand.

«Sperduta

in quella baraonda

lasciai qualche parola

come fa l'acqua del mare

col movimento dell'onda»:

Corbeilles de mariages

gerbes et couronnes.

abricots fondants

les bonnes fraises de Lion

poires au couteau

Pierrot gourmand.

"Lost

in that chaos

I left words

as waves throw off

their mist upon the sea":

Corbeilles de mariages

gerbes et couronnes.

The Twilight Poets

Sergio Corazzini

Sergio Corazzini was born in Rome in 1886 and lived a brief and difficult life. From youth he suffered from tuberculosis and, because of his family's financial hardships, had to leave school and work for an insurance company. He began publishing his poetry at the age of sixteen. His collections are *Dolcezze* (1904; "Sweetness") and *Piccolo libro inutile* (1906; "Little Useless Book")—which contains his best-known and quintessential poem "Desolazione del povero poeta sentimentale" ("Desolation of the Poor Sentimental Poet"). He succumbed to tuberculosis in Rome at the age of twenty-one. With Gozzano, Corazzini was a significant contributor to the twilight movement. Accordingly, his poetry (mostly free-verse) is melancholic and regressive; its common themes are alienation and mortality.

Desolazione del povero poeta sentimentale

I

Perché tu mi dici poeta?

Io non sono un poeta.

Io non sono che un piccolo fanciullo che piange.

Vedi: non ho che lagrime da offrire al Silenzio.

Perché tu mi dici: poeta?

II

Le mie tristezze sono povere tristezze comuni.

Le mie gioie furono semplici,

semplici così, che se io dovessi confessarle a te arrossirei.

Oggi io penso a morire.

III

Io voglio morire, solamente, perché sono stanco;

solamente perché i grandi angioli

su le vetrate delle catedrali

mi fanno tremare d'amore e di angoscia;

solamente perché, io sono, oramai,

rassegnato come uno specchio,

come un povero specchio melanconico.

Vedi che io non sono un poeta:

sono un fanciullo triste che ha voglia di morire.

IV

Oh, non maravigliarti della mia tristezza!

E non domandarmi;

Desolation of the Poor Sentimental Poet

I

Why do you say I am a poet?

I'm not a poet.

I'm nothing but a little boy who cries.

You see, I have nothing but tears to offer Silence.

Why do you say I am a poet?

II

My sorrows are poor common sorrows.

My joys were simple, so simple that were I

to confess them to you I would blush.

Today I am thinking of dying.

III

I want to die because I'm tired;

simply because the enormous angels

on the stained-glass cathedral windows

make me tremble with love and desperation;

simply because I am already

resigned like a poor mirror,

a melancholy one.

See that I'm not a poet?

I am a sad boy wishing to die.

IV

Don't be surprised at my pain!

And do not question me;

io non saprei dirti che parole così vane,

Dio mio, così vane,

che mi verrebbe di piangere come se fossi per morire.

Le mie lagrime avrebbero l'aria

di sgranare un rosario di tristezza

davanti alla mia anima sette volte dolente

ma io non sarei un poeta;

sarei, semplicemente, un dolce e pensoso fanciullo

cui avvenisse di pregare, così, come canta e come dorme.

V

Io mi comunico del silenzio, cotidianamente, come di Gesù.

E i sacerdoti del silenzio sono i romori,

poi che senza di essi io non avrei cercato e trovato il Dio.

VI

Questa notte ho dormito con le mani in croce.

Mi sembrò di essere un piccolo e dolce fanciullo

dimenticato da tutti gli umani,

povera tenera preda del primo venuto;

e desiderai di essere venduto,

di essere battuto

di esser costretto a digiunare

per potermi mettere a piangere tutto solo,

disperatamente triste, in un angolo oscuro.

VII

Io amo la vita semplice delle cose.

Quante passioni vidi sfogliarsi, a poco a poco,

I would tell you words so vain,

my God, so vain that I would start crying

as if I were about to die.

My tears would seem

to say their beads of sadness

in front of my soul of seven sorrows

but I would not be a poet;

I would simply be a sweet and brooding boy

who takes to prayer like to song and sleep.

V

I take silence in as I do Jesus.

Noise is the new guru of silence

that made me seek out and find God.

VI

Last night I slept with my hands crossed.

It seemed to me I was a sweet young boy

forgotten by the world,

a small, tender prey to anyone;

I wanted to be sold,

beaten, and forced to fast

so I could cry all alone

in a dark corner,

immeasurably sad.

VII

I love the simple life of things.

How many passions I have seen eroding

per ogni cosa che se ne andava!

Ma tu non mi comprendi e sorridi.

E pensi che io sia malato.

VIII

Oh, io sono, veramente malato!

E muoio, un poco, ogni giorno.

Vedi: come le cose.

Non sono, dunque, un poeta:

io so che per esser detto: poeta, conviene

viver ben altra vita!

Io non so, Dio mio, che morire.

Amen.

for each thing that no longer was!

But you don't understand me;

you smile and think that I am sick.

VIII

Oh yes, I'm truly sick!

I die a little every day.

You see, just as things do.

So, I am not a poet:

I know that to be called a poet

one must live quite a different life!

Dear God, I only know

how to die. So be it.

GUIDO GOZZANO

Guido Gozzano was born in Turin in 1883 into an aristocratic family. He originally planned to become a lawyer but gave up his studies for poetry and in 1907 published his first collection, *La via del rifugio* ("The Path to Shelter"), which was followed by his most recognized volume, *I colloqui* (1911; "Conversations"). Like Corazzini, Gozzano contracted tuberculosis and suffered from the disease for many years before dying in his birth town in 1916. His twilight poems express an ambivalent and ironic rapport with his surroundings. Although Gozzano had a brief encounter with religion toward the end of his life, resignation, illness, and self-destruction are frequent topoi in his work—in particular in the poem "Totò Merúmeni." In Gozzano, uncultivated gardens and uninhabited mansions remind the poetic narrator that the past is irretrievable and that death is looming.

Totò Merúmeni

I

Col suo giardino incolto, le sale vaste, i bei
balconi secentisti guarniti di verzura,
la villa sembra tolta da certi versi miei,
sembra la villa-tipo, del Libro di Lettura...

Pensa migliori giorni la villa triste, pensa
gaie brigate sotto gli alberi centenari,
banchetti illustri nella sala da pranzo immensa
e danze nel salone spoglio da gli antiquari.

Ma dove in altri tempi giungeva Casa Ansaldo,
Casa Rattazzi, Casa d'Azeglio, Casa Oddone,
s'arresta un'automobile fremendo e sobbalzando,
villosi forestieri picchiano la gorgòne.

S'ode un latrato e un passo, si schiude cautamente
la porta... In quel silenzio di chiostro e di caserma
vive Totò Merúmeni con una madre inferma,
una prozia canuta ed uno zio demente.

II

Totò ha venticinque anni, tempra sdegnosa,
molta cultura e gusto in opere d'inchiostro,

Totò Merúmeni; or, The Auto-Flagellant

I

With its neglected garden, its grandiose rooms, the lovely
rococo balconies all garnished with greenery,
the villa seems to have sprung out from some lines
of mine: the model in a Reading Primer.

The villa sadly thinks of better days,
of merry parties under century-old trees,
illustrious banquets in the huge dining room,
dances in the great hall fleeced by art dealers.

But where in former times the Ansaldos came,
the Oddones, the Rattazzis, the d'Azeglios,
now shaking and rattling a car whines to a halt,
and fur-decked aliens rap on the Gorgon knocker.

A bark sounds, then a step, then gingerly a door
is opened . . . In a silence of barracks and cloisters
lives Totò Merúmeni with a mother who's in pain,
a hoary great-aunt, and an uncle who's insane.

II

Totò is a haughty twenty-five-year-old
with plenty of culture and taste in penned works,

The poem is a self-portrait based on *Heautontimorumenos* ("The Auto-Flagellant"), by
the Latin poet Terence.

scarso cervello, scarsa morale, spaventosa
chiaroveggenza: è il vero figlio del tempo nostro.

Non ricco, giunta l'ora di «vender parolette»
(il suo Petrarca!...) e farsi baratto o gazzettiere,
Totò scelse l'esilio. E in libertà riflette
ai suoi trascorsi che sarà bello tacere.

Non è cattivo. Manda soccorso di danaro
al povero, all'amico un cesto di primizie;
non è cattivo. A lui ricorre lo scolaro
pel tema, l'emigrante per le commendatizie.

Gelido, consapevole di sé e dei suoi torti,
non è cattivo. È il *buono* che derideva il Nietzsche
«... in verità derido l'inetto che si dice
buono, perché non ha l'ugne abbastanza forti...»

Dopo lo studio grave, scende in giardino, gioca
coi suoi dolci compagni sull'erba che l'invita;
i suoi compagni sono: una ghiandaia roca,
un micio, una bertuccia che ha nome Makakita...

        III
La Vita si ritolse tutte le sue promesse.

Egli sognò per anni l'Amore che non venne,
sognò pel suo martirio attrici e principesse
ed oggi ha per amante la cuoca diciottenne.

small brain and morals, foresight not worth a dime:
he is the true son of our time.

Poor, when the moment came to "deal in words"
(as Petrarch calls it) and turn newsman or swindler,
Totò chose exile. In his freedom he ponders
past deeds that we'd better ignore.

He's not bad. He sends money to the destitute,
and to his friend a basket of fresh fruit.
He's not bad: students want his compositions;
immigrants ask him for recommendations.

Aloof and conscious of himself and his flaws,
he's not bad; rather, he's *the nice man* spurned
by Nietzsche: "Truly I do abhor the worm
who thinks he's good because he has no claws . . ."

After his in-depth studies, to the lawn he careens
to play with his dear friends on the inviting green.
His friends are a raucous jay, a cat,
and a monkey whose name is Makakeet.

III

Life reneged on its promises. He sighed
many years for a love that never arrived.
He dreamed to his torment of the stars and the princess;
today the eighteen-year-old cook is his mistress.

Quando la casa dorme, la giovinetta scalza,

fresca come una prugna al gelo mattutino,

giunge nella sua stanza, lo bacia in bocca, balza

su lui che la possiede, beato e resupino...

IV

Totò non può sentire. Un lento male indomo

inaridì le fonti prime del sentimento;

l'analisi e il sofisma fecero di quest'uomo

ciò che le fiamme fanno d'un edificio al vento.

Ma come le ruine che già seppero il fuoco

esprimono i giaggioli dai bei vividi fiori,

quell'anima riarsa esprime a poco a poco

una fiorita d'esili versi consolatori...

V

Così Totò Merúmeni, dopo tristi vicende,

quasi è felice. Alterna l'indagine e la rima.

Chiuso in se stesso, medita, s'accresce, esplora, intende

la vita dello Spirito che non intese prima.

Perché la voce è poca, e l'arte prediletta

immensa, perché il Tempo—mentre ch'io parlo!—va,

Totò opra in disparte, sorride, e meglio aspetta.

E vive. Un giorno è nato. Un giorno morirà.

When the house is asleep, the barefoot fawn,

fresh as a plum in the cool of the dawn,

enters his room, kisses him on the lips,

leaps on him who takes her, passive in bliss.

IV

Totò can't feel. A slow, fatal chill

to the primal springs of his soul brought ill;

sophistry and analysis did the man in

the way fires do a building in the wind.

But just as ruins beset by flames

put out irises with purple manes,

his parched spirit little by little shines

with a sparse flowering of soothing lines.

V

So Totò Merúmeni, after an unhappy search,

is almost happy. He goes from rhyme to research.

Closed in his shell, he ponders, grows, explores,

understands the Soul's life, which he never got before.

Since his voice is tiny, and the beloved art immense,

since Time—even as I babble on—goes by,

Totò works apart and smiles, and hopes for recompense.

He lives on. One day he was born. One day he will die.

La Signorina Felicita ovvero la Felicità

I

Signorina Felicita, a quest'ora
scende la sera nel giardino antico
della tua casa. Nel mio cuore amico
scende il ricordo. E ti rivedo ancora,
e Ivrea rivedo e la cerulea Dora
e quel dolce paese che non dico.

Signorina Felicita, è il tuo giorno!
A quest'ora che fai? Tosti il caffè
e il buon aroma si diffonde intorno?
O cuci i lini e canti e pensi a me,
all'avvocato che non fa ritorno?
E l'avvocato è qui: che pensa a te.

Pensa i bei giorni d'un autunno addietro,
Vill'Amarena a sommo dell'ascesa
coi suoi ciliegi e con la sua Marchesa
dannata, e l'orto dal profumo tetro
di busso e i cocci innumeri di vetro
sulla cinta vetusta, alla difesa...

Vill'Amarena! Dolce la tua casa
in quella grande pace settembrina!
La tua casa che veste una cortina

Miss Felicity

I

Miss Felicity, at this hour the evening

enfolds the ancient garden of your house.

Memory steals into my open heart.

And I see you again, and see Ivrea,

the deep blue Dora,[1]

and that hamlet that is so sweet to me.

What are you doing right now? It is your day,

Miss Felicity! Are you making coffee and

is its fresh aroma wafting all around?

Or are you sewing linens, singing, thinking

of me, the lawyer who does not return?

The lawyer's here and thinking of you.

He thinks of mild days of a bygone Fall,

Villa Amarena perched upon the slope

with cherry trees and its Marquise (God curse her),

its garden with its moldy smell

of boxwood and the million shards on top

of the ancient wall, so to defend it . . .

Villa Amarena! Your house was so sweet

in that immense September peace!

Your house that's wearing a maize curtain

---

[1] Ivrea is a town in Piedmont, in northern Italy. The Dora is its river.

di granoturco fino alla cimasa:

come una dama secentista, invasa

dal Tempo, che vestì da contadina.

Bell'edificio triste inabitato!

Grate panciute, logore, contorte!

Silenzio! Fuga delle stanze morte!

Odore d'ombra! Odore di passato!

Odore d'abbandono desolato!

Fiabe defunte delle sovrapporte!

Ercole furibondo ed il Centauro,

le gesta dell'eroe navigatore,

Fetonte e il Po, lo sventurato amore

d'Arianna, Minosse, il Minotauro,

Dafne rincorsa, trasmutata in lauro

tra le braccia del Nume ghermitore...

Penso l'arredo—che malinconia!—

penso l'arredo squallido e severo,

antico e nuovo: la pirografia

sui divani corinzi dell'Impero,

la cartolina della Bella Otero

alle specchiere... Che malinconia!

up to the cornice—like a seventeenth-
   century lady who, beleaguered
by Time, dressed like a peasant.

Fanciful, sad, uninhabited building!
Worn, paunchy, twisted gratings!
Silence! Flight of dead rooms!
Smell of the past! Of gloom!
Smell of dejected desolation!
The stormdoors' dried-up fabrications!

Hercules run amok and the Centaur,
the feats of the navigator hero,[2]
Phaeton and the Po River, Ariadne's
tragic affair, Minos, the Minotaur,
Daphne pursued and turned into a laurel
in the god's grasping arms . . .[3]

I think of the interiors—what tristesse!—
the austere, squalid decor,
ancient and new: the fire-engraved friezes
on the Corinthian sofas,[4] "mode Empire,"
and inside mirror frames Lovely Otero's
picture[5] . . . Oh, what tristesse!

---

[2] The navigator hero is Ulysses.
[3] The god is Apollo.
[4] The sofas are decorated with capitals in the Corinthian style.
[5] Lovely Otero is a well-known fin de siècle ballerina.

Antica suppellettile forbita!

Armadi immensi pieni di lenzuola

che tu rammendi pazïente... Avita

semplicità che l'anima consola,

semplicità dove tu vivi sola

con tuo padre la tua semplice vita!

II

Quel tuo buon padre—in fama d'usuraio—

quasi bifolco, m'accoglieva senza

inquietarsi della mia frequenza,

mi parlava dell'uve e del massaio,

mi confidava certo antico guaio

notarile, con somma deferenza.

«Senta, avvocato...» e mi traeva inquieto

nel salone, talvolta, con un atto

che leggeva lentissimo, in segreto.

Io l'ascoltavo docile, distratto

da quell'odor d'inchiostro putrefatto,

da quel disegno strano sul tappeto,

da quel salone buio e troppo vasto...

«...La Marchesa fuggì... Le spese cieche...»

da quel parato a ghirlandette, a greche...

«dell'ottocento e dieci, ma il catasto...»

da quel tic-tac dell'orologio guasto...

«...l'ipotecario è morto, e l'ipoteche...»

Old polished furnishings!

Huge armoires filled with sheets

that you patiently darn . . . Ancestral modesty

that warms the soul, simplicity

where with no complications, all alone,

you live your life with Father!

II

That good father of yours, reputed stingy,

somewhat boorish, welcomed me without getting

upset by my numerous calls; he told me

about grapes and his farmer, trusted me

with an old legal matter

in a most courteous manner.

"Hear me, sir . . ." and he'd worriedly draw me

at times into the spacious sitting room

with a deed he read very slowly, in secret.

Submissively, I would listen to him,

distracted by the smell of musty ink,

by the peculiar pattern on the rug,

by that dark, too vast room . . .

". . . the Marquise fled. Incredible expenses . . ."

that tapestry all garlands and Greek frets . . .

". . . from eighteen-hundred-and-ten, but the land office . . ."

by the ticktock of the out-of-order clock . . .

". . . the mortgage lender's dead, the mortgages . . ."

Capiva poi che non capivo niente
e sbigottiva: «Ma l'ipotecario
è morto, è morto!» — «E se l'ipotecario
è morto, allora...» Fortunatamente
tu comparivi tutta sorridente:
«Ecco il nostro malato immaginario!»

III

Sei quasi brutta, priva di lusinga
nelle tue vesti quasi campagnole,
ma la tua faccia buona e casalinga,
ma i bei capelli di color di sole,
attorti in minutissime trecciuole,
ti fanno un tipo di beltà fiamminga...

E rivedo la tua bocca vermiglia
così larga nel ridere e nel bere,
e il volto quadro, senza sopracciglia,
tutto sparso d'efelidi leggiere
e gli occhi fermi, l'iridi sincere
azzurre d'un azzurro di stoviglia...

Tu m'hai amato. Nei begli occhi fermi
rideva una blandizie femminina.
Tu civettavi con sottili schermi,
tu volevi piacermi, Signorina:
e più d'ogni conquista cittadina
mi lusingò quel tuo voler piacermi!

Then he realized
I hadn't got one word
and stammered: "But the mortgage lender's dead,
dead! . . ."—"So, if the mortgage lender's dead,
then . . ." Fortunately you arrived
all smiles: "How's Mr. Faker?"

III

You're almost ugly, devoid of allure
in your close-to-plain country dresses,
but your good-natured, homely face
and your sun-colored pretty tresses,
twisted and turned into thin braids,
cast you as a kind of Flemish belle . . .

And I see your vermilion mouth again
so wide when laughing and when drinking,
square face with no eyelashes,
dotted with tiny freckles,
the steady eyes, the sincere irises
blue like blue china . . .

You did love me. In your beautiful gaze
shone an all-feminine enchantment.
You flirted with naive endearments
and wanted me to like you, Miss:
and more than any city conquest
how your wanting to please me flattered me!

Ogni giorno salivo alla tua volta
pel soleggiato ripido sentiero.
Il farmacista non pensò davvero
un'amicizia così bene accolta,
quando ti presentò la prima volta
l'ignoto villeggiante forestiero.

Talora—già la mensa era imbandita—
mi trattenevi a cena. Era una cena
d'altri tempi, col gatto e la falena
e la stoviglia semplice e fiorita
e il commento dei cibi e Maddalena
decrepita, e la siesta e la partita...

Per la partita, verso ventun'ore
giungeva tutto l'inclito collegio
politico locale: il molto Regio
Notaio, il signor Sindaco, il Dottore;
ma—poiché trasognato giocatore—
quei signori m'avevano in dispregio...

M'era più dolce starmene in cucina
tra le stoviglie a vividi colori:
tu tacevi, tacevo, Signorina.
Godevo quei silenzi e quegli odori
tanto tanto per me consolatori,
di basilico d'aglio di cedrina...

Every day I used to climb your way
up the steep, sunny path.
The druggist never could have thought
my friendship so warmly received
when he first introduced
the out-of-town vacationer to you.

Once in a while—with the food all laid out—
you kept me at dinner. And it was a dinner
of long ago, cat and moth in the picture,
the simple flower-painted dishes,
and comments about food, doddering Maggie,
then the siesta, the game . . .

At about 9 p.m.
the whole eminent town
body politic gathered for the game—
the illustrious Notary, the Doctor, the Mayor.
But I was absent-minded as a player,
and so those celebs held me in contempt.

I much preferred to curl up in the kitchen
among the brightly colored dishes:
I was silent and you, young lady, too.
I enjoyed that silence and the smell
of basil, garlic, and verbena so
soothing to my heart while Magdalen

Maddalena con sordo brontolio

disponeva gli arredi ben detersi,

rigovernava lentamente ed io,

già smarrito nei sogni più diversi,

accordavo le sillabe dei versi

sul ritmo eguale dell'acciotolio.

Sotto l'immensa cappa del camino

(in me rivive l'anima d'un cuoco

forse...) godevo il sibilo del fuoco;

la canzone d'un grillo canterino

mi diceva parole, a poco a poco,

e vedevo Pinocchio e il mio destino...

Vedevo questa vita che m'avanza:

chiudevo gli occhi nei presagi grevi;

aprivo gli occhi: tu mi sorridevi,

ed ecco rifioriva la speranza!

Giungevano le risa, i motti brevi

dei giocatori, da quell'altra stanza.

IV

Bellezza riposata dei solai

dove il rifiuto secolare dorme!

In quella tomba, tra le vane forme

di ciò ch'è stato e non sarà più mai,

bianca bella così che sussultai,

la Dama apparve nella tela enorme:

mumbling dully would put the serving bowls
back after cleaning them then slowly do
the dishes. I, already lost
in the most varied dreams,
set my lines' scansions to
the even rhythm of the wash.

Under the big cowl of the fireplace
(perhaps a cook's soul lives anew in me . . .)
I enjoyed the hissing of the fire;
a singing cricket's chirps
bit by bit became words—
I saw Pinocchio and my fate . . .

I saw the life that lay ahead;
closed my eyes in gloomy forebodings;
opened them: you were smiling at me,
and hope again was blooming.
Laughter, and the players' repartees,
got to us from the other room.

IV

O restful beauty of the attics where
the discards of the centuries lie dormant!
And in that grave, among the formless shapes
of what was once and never will be again,
so white and lovely that I shook,
the lady appeared on an enormous canvas:

«È quella che lasciò, per infortuni,
la casa al nonno di mio nonno... E noi
la confinammo nel solaio, poi
che porta pena... L'han veduta alcuni
lasciare il quadro; in certi noviluni
s'ode il suo passo lungo i corridoi...»

Il nostro passo diffondeva l'eco
tra quei rottami del passato vano,
e la Marchesa dal profilo greco,
altocinta, l'un piede ignudo in mano,
si riposava all'ombra d'uno speco
arcade, sotto un bel cielo pagano.

Intorno a quella che rideva illusa
nel ricco peplo, e che morì di fame,
v'era una stirpe logora e confusa:
topaie, materassi, vasellame,
lucerne, ceste, mobili: ciarpame
reietto, così caro alla mia Musa!

Tra i materassi logori e le ceste
v'erano stampe di persone egregie;
incoronato delle frondi regie
v'era *Torquato nei giardini d'Este.*
«Avvocato, perché su quelle teste
buffe si vede un ramo di ciliegie?»

"She is the one who, hit by bad luck, left

the house to my grandpa's grandfather . . . We

confined her to the attic, since she is

a sad sight. Some have seen her leave the painting;

sometimes, when the moon is new, her steps

can be heard in the halls . . ."

Our steps would send the echo

across the flotsam of the useless past;

Greek-profiled and high-waisted, the Marquise,

holding her bare foot in one hand,

lay resting in the shade of an Arcadian

cave, under a limpid pagan sky.

Around the one who tittered in her rich

peplum and who, deluded, died of hunger,

was a confused and tattered host—

rat nests, mattresses, pottery,

furniture, hampers, lamps: the abject junk

my muse cherishes so!

Among the frayed hampers and pads

stood prints of renowned lads:

decked out in regal fronds

was our *Torquato in the Este Gardens*.

"Mr. Attorney, what are the cherry garlands

for on those funny heads?"

Io risi, tanto che fermammo il passo,
e ridendo pensai questo pensiero:
Oimé! La Gloria! un corridoio basso,
tre ceste, un canterano dell'Impero,
la brutta effigie incorniciata in nero
e sotto il nome di Torquato Tasso!

Allora, quasi a voce che richiama,
esplorai la pianura autunnale
dall'abbaino secentista, ovale,
a telaietti fitti, ove la trama
del vetro deformava il panorama
come un antico smalto innaturale.

Non vero (e bello) come in uno smalto
a zone quadre, apparve il Canavese:
Ivrea turrita, i colli di Montalto,
la Serra dritta, gli alberi, le chiese;
e il mio sogno di pace si protese
da quel rifugio luminoso ed alto.

Ecco—pensavo—questa è l'Amarena,
ma laggiù, oltre i colli dilettosi,
c'è il Mondo: quella cosa tutta piena
di lotte e di commerci turbinosi,
la cosa tutta piena di quei «cosi
con due gambe» che fanno tanta pena...

I laughed so hard we had to stop our walk,
and, while laughing, I entertained this thought:
Glory, alas! a low corridor, three hampers,
a chest of drawers dating from the Empire,
an ugly portrait all in jet-black wreathed
with the name Torquato Tasso underneath!

Then, as if drawn by a refrain,
I took to exploring
the autumnal plain
from the rococo oval of the dormer
all framed with lattice, whose glass pane deformed
the vista like an odd, ancient enamel.

Not true (though charming) as in an enamel
in square patterns appeared the Canavese:
Ivrea and her towers, the Montalto Hills,
the straight Serra,[6] the churches, and the trees—
my dream of peace stretched farther
from that high, shining shelter.

Right here—I thought—is Amarena, but
yonder, beyond the basking ridges,
is the World: that thing so full of strife
and hectic trade, that thing all full of those
"two-legged creatures"
that distress me so . . .

---

[6] The Montalto Hills and the Serra are parts of the Ivrea landscape.

L'Eguagliatrice numera le fosse,
ma quelli vanno, spinti da chimere
vane, divisi e suddivisi a schiere
opposte, intesi all'odio e alle percosse:
così come ci son formiche rosse,
così come ci son formiche nere...

Schierati al sole o all'ombra della Croce,
tutti travolge il turbine dell'oro;
o Musa—oimé!—che può giovare loro
il ritmo della mia piccola voce?
Meglio fuggire dalla guerra atroce
del piacere, dell'oro, dell'alloro...

L'alloro... Oh! Bimbo semplice che fui,
dal cuore in mano e dalla fronte alta!
Oggi l'alloro è premio di colui
che tra clangor di buccine s'esalta,
che sale cerretano alla ribalta
per far di sé favoleggiare altrui...

«Avvocato, non parla: che cos'ha?»
«Oh! Signorina! Penso ai casi miei,
a piccole miserie, alla città...
Sarebbe dolce restar qui, con Lei!...»—
«Qui, nel solaio?...»—«Per l'eternità!»—
«Per sempre? Accetterebbe?...»—"Accetterei!»

The Equalizer allocates the graves,[7]
but men push on, driven by foolish dreams,
divided, subdivided into clashing
rows bent on hateful blows:
the way red ants
oppose black warriors . . .

Marshaled under the sun, or by God dimmed,
the whorl of gold sucks everybody in;
damn it, O Muse, what use
is the rhythm of my puny voice to them?
Better to flee from the horrendous mayhem
of pleasure, laurels, and of gold . . .

Laurels . . . Oh, times I was a simple boy,
with my heart on my sleeve, my head held high!
Today that laurel is the prize for him
who by the blare of trumpets is elated,
who walks like any fraud up to the stage
to have the mob in flattery engage . . .

"Mr. Attorney: you don't speak. You're ill?"
"Oh, Miss. I was just thinking of my troubles,
little chagrins, the city . . . What a thrill
it would be instead to stay right here with you! . . ."—
"Here, in the attic? . . ."—"Yes, for all eternity!"—
"Forever? Would you accept? . . ."—"Don't you ever doubt it!"

---

[7] The Equalizer is Death.

Tacqui. Scorgevo un atropo soletto
e prigioniero. Stavasi in riposo
alla parete: il segno spaventoso
chiuso tra l'ali ripiegate a tetto.

Come lo vellicai sul corsaletto
si librò con un ronzo lamentoso.

«Che ronzo triste!»—«È la Marchesa in pianto...
La Dannata sarà che porta pena.»
Nulla s'udiva che la sfinge in pena
e dalle vigne, ad ora ad ora, un canto:

O mio carino tu mi piaci tanto,
siccome piace al mar una sirena...

Un richiamo s'alzò, querulo e roco:
«È Maddalena inquieta che si tardi;
scendiamo; è l'ora della cena!»—«Guardi,
guardi il tramonto, là. Com'è di fuoco!...
Restiamo ancora un poco!»—«Andiamo, è tardi!»
«Signorina, restiamo ancora un poco!...»

Le fronti al vetro, chini sulla piana,
seguimmo i neri pipistrelli, a frotte;
giunse col vento un ritmo di campana,
disparve il sole fra le nubi rotte;
a poco a poco s'annunciò la notte
sulla serenità canavesana...

I fell silent. I watched an *Atropos*
that had been trapped.[8] It was resting on the wall—
the mark of death embossed beneath the wings
folded just like a roof.
As I tickled its corselet, it flew off
with a lamenting hum.

"What a sad sound!"—"It's the weeping Marquise . . .
It must be her damned soul dragging its chain . . ."
Nothing was heard but the sorrowing sphynx,
and from the vineyards now and then a song:
I love you so much, my beloved,
the way the sea loves a mermaid . . .

A call rang out, querulous, like a bray:
"It's Magdalen, worried that we delay;
let's down; it's supper time!"—"Look at the sunset
over there, look! Bright flames of scarlet! . . .
Let's stay here longer!"—"We must go; make haste!"
"Miss, a bit longer! . . ." With our forehead pressed

against the glass, overlooking the plain,
we followed the formations of black bats;
commingled with the wind the bell's toll came;
then the sun vanished behind tattered clouds
and bit by bit the night announced itself
on the serenity of the Canavese.

---

[8] The atropos butterfly has a head shaped like the Sphinx.

«Una stella!...»—«Tre stelle!...»—«Quattro stelle!...»

«Cinque stelle!»—«Non sembra di sognare?...»

Ma ti levasti su quasi ribelle

alla perplessità crepuscolare:

«Scendiamo! È tardi: possono pensare

che noi si faccia cose poco belle...»

V

Ozi beati a mezzo la giornata,

nel parco dei Marchesi, ove la traccia

restava appena dell'età passata!

Le Stagioni camuse e senza braccia,

fra mucchi di letame e di vinaccia,

dominavano i porri e l'insalata.

L'insalata, i legumi produttivi

deridevano il busso delle aiole;

volavano le pieridi nel sole

e le cetonie e i bombi fuggitivi...

Io ti parlavo piano, e tu cucivi

inebriata delle mie parole.

«Tutto mi spiace che mi piacque innanzi!

Ah! Rimanere qui, sempre, al suo fianco,

terminare la vita che m'avanzi

tra questo verde e questo lino bianco!

Se lei sapesse come sono stanco

delle donne rifatte sui romanzi!

"One star! . . ."—"Three stars! . . ."—"One more appeared! . . ."
"Five!"—"Doesn't it seem unreal? . . ."
But you arose, almost ready to fight
against the uncertain twilight:
"Let's go down! It is late: they may think we
are doing something that we shouldn't do . . ."

V

Blessed lulls in the middle of the day
in the Marquise's park, where only a trace
of the past age remained!
Some pug-nosed, armless Seasons
among the heaps of compost and grape pressings
dominated the salad and the leeks.

The salad and the multiplying greens
mocked the boxwood laid in their flowerbeds;
butterflies were aflutter in the sun
with beetles and the fleeting bumblebees . . .
I was talking to you, softly; you were
sewing, enchanted by my words.

"Whatever I first liked is now displeasure!
Ah! To stay here right by your side forever;
to finish my remaining life
between the green and this white linen!
If you only knew how tired I've become
of women patterned on romances!

Vennero donne con proteso il cuore:
ognuna dileguò, senza vestigio.
Lei sola, forse, il freddo sognatore
educherebbe al tenero prodigio:
mai non comparve sul mio cielo grigio
quell'aurora che dicono l'Amore.»

Tu mi fissavi: nei begli occhi fissi
leggevo uno sgomento indefinito;
le mani ti cercai, sopra il cucito,
e te le strinsi lungamente, e dissi:
«Mia cara Signorina, se guarissi
ancora, mi vorrebbe per marito?»

«Perché mi fa tali discorsi vani?
Sposare, Lei, me brutta e poveretta!...»
E ti piegasti sulla tua panchetta
facendo al viso coppa delle mani,
simulando singhiozzi acuti e strani
per celia, come fa la scolaretta.

Ma nel chinarmi su di te, m'accorsi
che sussultavi come chi singhiozza
veramente, né sa più ricomporsi:
mi parve udire la tua voce mozza
dagli ultimi singulti nella strozza:
«Non mi ten...ga mai più tali dis...corsi!»

There came ladies, their hearts on display:
they all vanished, and nothing has stayed.
Only you, perhaps, could lead the cold
dreamer to that devoted portent:
in my gray sky that dawn called Love
never appeared . . ."

You stared at me . . . In your beautiful stare
I read an undeciphered fright;
over the sewing I looked for your hands
and squeezed them long, then said:
"My dear young Lady, if I ever recovered
how would you like to take me for your husband?"

"Why do you speak lightheartedly to me?
You marry me, ugly and without a penny! . . ."
And you hunched over your small bench,
hiding your face inside your hands,
faking shrill and strange cries
in jest, the way a student does.

But in bending toward you I realized
that you were shaking just like one who shakes
for real and can no longer stop herself:
I thought I heard your voice half choked
by the sobs in your throat:
"Don't you ever dare . . . speak to me . . . like that!"

«Piange?» E tentai di sollevarti il viso

inutilmente. Poi, colto un fuscello,

ti vellicai l'orecchio, il collo snello...

Già tutta luminosa nel sorriso

ti sollevasti vinta d'improvviso,

trillando un trillo gaio di fringuello.

Donna: mistero senza fine bello!

VI

Tu m'hai amato. Nei begli occhi fermi

luceva una blandizie femminina;

tu civettavi con sottili schermi,

tu volevi piacermi, Signorina;

e più d'ogni conquista cittadina

mi lusingò quel tuo voler piacermi!

Unire la mia sorte alla tua sorte

per sempre, nella casa centenaria!

Ah! Con te, forse, piccola consorte

vivace, trasparente come l'aria,

rinnegherei la fede letteraria

che fa la vita simile alla morte...

Oh! questa vita sterile, di sogno!

Meglio la vita ruvida concreta

del buon mercante inteso alla moneta,

meglio andare sferzati dal bisogno,

ma vivere di vita! Io mi vergogno,

sì, mi vergogno d'essere un poeta!

"Are you crying?" And uselessly I tried
to lift your face. Then, with a blade of grass
I tickled your ear, your slender neck . . .
Already all shining with your smile
you stood up, no more to contend,
warbling the happy warble of a finch.
Woman: a mystery, charming without end!

VI

You loved me. In your beautiful gaze
an all-feminine rapture blazed;
you flirted from behind thin screens;
you wanted me to like you, Signorina:
and more than any city conquest
your wanting to please me was so endearing!

Ah! To conjoin my destiny with yours
forever, in this ancient house!
Perhaps with you at my side, my little lively
bride transparent as air,
I would renounce my literary faith
that makes life similar to death . . .

Oh! the sterility of this bloodless life!
Better the concrete, raw existence
of the good merchant keen on money;
better to move, whipped on by need,
but live for real! I so regret,
yes, I do, being a poet!

Tu non fai versi. Tagli le camicie

per tuo padre. Hai fatto la seconda

classe, t'han detto che la Terra è tonda,

ma tu non credi. E non mediti Nietzsche...

Mi piaci. Mi faresti più felice

d'un'intellettuale gemebonda...

Tu ignori questo male che s'apprende

in noi. Tu vivi i tuoi giorni modesti,

tutta beata nelle tue faccende.

Mi piaci. Penso che leggendo questi

miei versi tuoi, non mi comprenderesti,

ed a me piace chi non mi comprende.

Ed io non voglio più essere io!

VII

Il farmacista nella farmacia

m'elogiava un farmaco sagace:

«Vedrà che dorme le sue notti in pace:

un sonnifero d'oro, in fede mia!»

Narrava, intanto, certa gelosia

con non so che loquacità mordace.

«Ma c'è il notaio pazzo di quell'oca!

Ah! quel notaio, creda: un capo ameno!

La Signorina è brutta, senza seno,

volgaruccia, Lei sa, come una cuoca...

You do not write. You fashion shirts
for your father. You went to second grade;
they told you that the Earth is round—
you didn't buy it . . . You don't meditate
on Nietzsche . . . I like you. I would be happier bound
to you than to a dour bluestocking.

You do not know this evil that corrodes us.
You live your simple days, happily wrapped
up in your chores. I like you. I think that reading
these lines written for you
you wouldn't have a clue,
and I like those
who do not get my meaning.

And I no longer want to be myself!

    VII

The druggist in his pharmacy was praising
a clever remedy of his: "You'll see:
with this you'll sleep at night so peacefully—
a golden sleeping tablet, word of honor!"
In the meantime, he told me of a certain
intrigue, using somewhat caustic palaver.

"Take the notary, crazy for that bloop
of nature. He is quite a nincompoop!
The Miss is ugly and has tiny boobs;
she's a bit common, you know, just like a cook . . .

E la dote... la dote è poca, poca:

diecimila, chi sa, forse nemmeno...»

«Ma dunque?»—«C'è il notaio furibondo

con Lei, con me che volli presentarla

a Lei; non mi saluta, non mi parla...»—

«È geloso?»—«Geloso! Un finimondo!...»—

«Pettegolezzi!...»—«Ma non Le nascondo

che temo, temo qualche brutta ciarla...»—

«Non tema. Parto.»—«Parte? E va lontano?»—

«Molto lontano... Vede, cade a mezzo

ogni motivo di pettegolezzo...»—

«Davvero parte? Quando?»—«In settimana.»

Ed uscii dall'odor d'ipecacuana

nel plenilunio settembrino, al rezzo.

Andai vagando nel silenzio amico,

triste perduto come un mendicante.

Mezzanotte scoccò, lenta, rombante

su quel dolce paese che non dico.

La luna sopra il campanile antico

pareva «un punto sopra un I gigante.»

In molti mesti e pochi sogni lieti,

solo pellegrinai col mio rimpianto

fra le siepi, le vigne, i castagneti

And the dowery . . . the dowery's so small;
I'll bet ten thousand, if that after all . . ."

"So what?"—"Ah yes: the notary is mad
at you, at me who introduced her to
you; he doesn't say hello to me . . ."—
"Well—is he jealous?"—"Jealous? He is insane!"
"Old wives' tale! . . ."—"I'll be frank with you. I fear
some nasty gossip . . ."—"Please, do not. I'm leaving."—

"Leaving? And are you going very far?"—
"Very. So you can see
any reason for gossip disappears . . ."—
"Really, you're leaving? When?"—"Within this week."
I left behind the ipecacuanha's perfume
and faced the breezy full September moon.

I kept on wandering in the warm silence
gloomy and lost like a beggar. Midnight came,
like a slow rumble over our
hamlet that is so sweet to me.
The moon atop the ancient belfry tower
was like "a dot on a gigantic I."

In many heavy, very few light dreams,
I walked alone with my sad reveries
along the hedges, vineyards, chestnut woods

quasi d'argento fatti nell'incanto;

e al cancello sostai del camposanto

come s'usa nei libri dei poeti.

Voi che posate già sull'altra riva,

immuni dalla gioia, dallo strazio,

parlate, o morti, al pellegrino sazio!

Giova guarire? Giova che si viva?

O meglio giova l'Ospite furtiva

che ci affranca dal Tempo e dallo Spazio?

A lungo meditai, senza ritrarre

la tempia dalle sbarre. Quasi a scherno

s'udiva il grido delle strigi alterno...

La luna, prigioniera fra le sbarre,

imitava con sue luci bizzarre

gli amanti che si baciano in eterno.

Bacio lunare, fra le nubi chiare

come di moda settant'anni fa!

Ecco la Morte e la Felicità!

L'una m'incalza quando l'altra appare;

quella m'esilia in terra d'oltremare,

questa promette il bene che sarà...

VIII

Nel mestissimo giorno degli addii

mi piacque rivedere la tua villa.

in that spell made as if of silver;

and at the graveyard gate I lingered

the way they do in poets' books.

Already resting on the opposite shore,

no joy or harrowing pain for you in store:

speak, O you dead, to the world-weary pilgrim!

Is recovering worth it? Living more?

Or is the furtive guest that snatches us

from Time and Space much better?

I pondered at length, my forehead pressed

against the gate. And as in mockery

I heard the alternate screeching of the owls . . .

The moon, caught between bars,

mirrored with its uncanny luminosity

lovers kissing each other for eternity.

A moonlight kiss among the clouds aglow

as fashion had it seventy years ago!

Here's Happiness, and Death is over there!

One hounds me when the other does appear;

one exiles me to a land across the sea,

the other promises the good that will be . . .

    VIII

On the agonizing day of separation

I felt like visiting your villa again.

La morte dell'estate era tranquilla

in quel mattino chiaro che salii

tra i vigneti già spogli, tra i pendii

già trapunti di bei colchici lilla.

Forse vedendo il bel fiore malvagio

che i fiori uccide e semina le brume,

le rondini addestravano le piume

al primo volo, timido, randagio;

e a me randagio parve buon presagio

accompagnarmi loro nel costume.

«Vïaggio con le rondini stamane...»

«Dove andrà?»—«Dove andrò? non so... Vïaggio,

vïaggio per fuggire altro vïaggio...

Oltre Marocco, ad isolette strane,

ricche in essenze, in datteri, in banane,

perdute nell'Atlantico selvaggio...

Signorina, s'io torni d'oltremare,

non sarà d'altri già? Sono sicuro

di ritrovarla ancora? Questo puro

amore nostro salirà l'altare?»

E vidi la tua bocca sillabare

a poco a poco le sillabe: *giuro*.

Giurasti e disegnasti una ghirlanda

sul muro, di viole e di saette,

The death of summer was a mute refrain
on that clear morning when I walked
through the bare vineyards, on the slopes
already laced with lovely purple crocus.

Having perhaps seen the mean, pretty bloom
that kills the flowers and spreads mists,
swallows were training on the wing
for their first shy and rootless flight:
and to the rootless, it seemed a good thing
to join them in their plight.

"This morning I'll be leaving with the swallows . . ."
"Where will you go?"—"Where? I don't know. I go
and keep on going to escape the journey . . .
Beyond Morocco, to strange islands, tiny,
bestrewn with dates, bananas, rich spices,
marooned in the raging Atlantic . . .

Young lady, if I come back from overseas,
will you be someone else's? Am I sure
I'll find you again? And will this pure
love of ours get to the altar ever?"
I saw your mouth spell with the greatest care
the words: *I swear.*

You swore and on the wall you drew
a garland of violets and arrows

coi nomi e con la data memoranda:

trenta settembre novecentosette...

Io non sorrisi. L'animo godette

quel romantico gesto d'educanda.

Le rondini garrivano assordanti,

garrivano garrivano parole

d'addio, guizzando ratte come spole,

incitando le piccole migranti...

Tu seguivi gli stormi lontananti

ad uno ad uno per le vie del sole.

«Un altro stormo s'alza!...» — «Ecco s'avvia!»...

«Sono partite...» — «E non le salutò!...» —

«Lei devo salutare, quelle no:

quelle terranno la mia stessa via.

In un palmetto della Barberia

tra pochi giorni le ritroverò.»

Giunse il distacco, amaro senza fine,

e fu il distacco d'altri tempi, quando

le amate in bande lisce e in crinoline,

protese da un giardino venerando,

singhiozzavano forte, salutando

diligenze che andavano al confine...

M'apparisti così come in un cantico

del Prati, lacrimante l'abbandono

with our names and the memorable date:
September thirty nineteen hundred and seven . . .
I didn't smile. My soul acknowledged heaven
in that move, loving and sedate.

The din of swallows drummed into our ears;
they were chirping and chirping farewell throbbings,
whirling as fast as bobbins,
spurring on their migrating little ones . . .
You were following flights that one by one
disappeared on the paths of the sun.

"Another flock is rising!"—"There, it took off!"—
"They have left . . ."—"And you didn't say good-bye! . . ."—
"I must say good-bye to you, not them:
they are taking the path I'll take myself.
In a palmetto near Tunis in a few
days I'll see them again . . ."

The parting came, endlessly cruel,
and it was one of another era, when
the loved one, decked in crinoline, hair pulled
straight, peeking out from a dignified bower,
sobbed loudly and waved to coaches
bound for the border . . .

You appeared to me as in a song by Prati,
bewailing my departure for the lost

per l'isole perdute nell'Atlantico;

ed io fui l'uomo d'altri tempi, un buono

sentimentale giovine romantico...

Quello che fingo d'essere e non sono!

(pubblicata la prima volta nel 1909, il 10 luglio, festa di S. Felicita)

isles of the Atlantic;

I was a man from a different epoch,

an honest, young romantic sop . . .

What I pretend to be and am not!

(First published in 1909, on July 10, Saint Felicita)

Fausto Maria Martini

Fausto Maria Martini was born in Rome in 1886. He is best known as a novelist, critic, and playwright and is considered a minor contributor to the twilight movement. His three volumes of poetry are *Le piccole morte* (1906; "Les petites morts"), *Panem nostrum* (1907; "Our Daily Bread"), and *Poesie provinciali* (1910; "Provincial Poems"). Martini dedicated many of his verses to the twilight poet Corazzini and recalled his friendship with and admiration for him in his autobiographical novel *Si sbarca a New York* (1930; "We Disembark in New York"), which recounts his brief stay in New York City after Corazzini's death. Martini fought in World War I, where he was gravely wounded, and he died in Rome in 1931 as a result of his injuries. Many of his verses ("Annie," "La sfinge" ["The Sphinx"], and "Castità" ["Chastity"]) are erotic; in them woman is positioned as enigmatic and frequently tied to sensuality and death.

San Saba

(per Sergio Corazzini)

Sergio, e dicevi: «Ella ti vuole morto,
ti stringe ella in un suo gorgo soave...
tu non potrai, fratello, nel risorto
giorno, gridare al sol nascente l'Ave...»

Sergio, dicevi... Or io, nella pazzia
notturna, scaccio la mia mamma santa
come un'immonda... Perché non imprechi,
gonfia di mute lacrime, la mia
mamma si parte. Solo con l'affranta
anima, resto: ed ecco, in fondo ai biechi
cipressi brancolanti come ciechi,
tempio al suicida, con le cave grotte
d'ombra, San Saba, immensa nella notte...

Sergio, e dicevi... «Ella ti vuole morto...»

Saint Saba

For Sergio Corazzini

Sergio, you said: "She wants you dead,

she drowns you in her magnetic vortex . . .

Brother, you won't be allowed on resurrection

day to say prayers to the rising sun."

Sergio, you said. Now I in my nightmare

avoid my mother as if she were a leper.

And (lest I start blaspheming) she,

swollen with silent tears, departs.

I stay alone with my dejected soul.

Then, where grim cypress trees

end, groping like blind men,

a shrine to suicide, its niches all in shadow,

there looms Saint Saba, forbidding in the night.

Sergio, you said: "She wants you dead."

Saint Saba is a church in Rome.

Poets from *La voce*

CAMILLO SBARBARO

Camillo Sbarbaro was born in Santa Margherita Ligure in 1888 and in elementary school began writing poetry, which was published as *Resine* ("Resins") by his companions in 1911, followed by *Pianissimo* ("Softly") in 1914. He contributed to journals such as *La voce* ("The Voice") and *Lacerba*, and fought in World War I as a soldier and infantryman. He returned from the war disheartened and lived much of his life in seclusion, supporting himself by working as a tutor, translator, and botanist. He was re-·nowned for his lichen collection. Sbarbaro died in Savona in 1967. In his poems, the object is stripped down to its essentiality. In many of his earlier poems the landscape is desolate and unwelcoming, and the poetic narrator suffers from existential angst. In his later *Rimanenze* (1955; "Remnants"), however, the natural world has a somewhat conciliatory function.

Ora che sei venuta,...

Ora che sei venuta,

che con passo di danza sei entrata

nella mia vita

quasi folata in una stanza chiusa—

a festeggiarti, bene tanto atteso,

le parole mi mancano e la voce

e tacerti vicino già mi basta.

Il pigolío così che assorda il bosco

al nascere dell'alba, ammutolisce

quando sull'orizzonte balza il sole.

Ma te la mia inquietudine cercava

quando ragazzo

nella notte d'estate mi facevo

alla finestra come soffocato:

che non sapevo, m'affannava il cuore.

E tutte tue sono le parole

che, come l'acqua all'orlo che trabocca,

alla bocca venivano da sole,

l'ore deserte, quando s'avanzavan

puerilmente le mie labbra d'uomo

da sé, per desiderio di baciare...

Now that you've come . . .

Now that you've come and with a lilting step
entered my life, fresh air
in stuffy rooms, words and my voice do fail me
to welcome you, beloved long awaited,
and to be silent near you is enough:
like the chirping of birds that stuns the woods
as dawn arises, stops
when the sun leaps to the horizon.

But it was you my restlessness was seeking
when on a summer night, a boy, I came
to the window. I was choking
and didn't know it was my young heart breaking.
And all yours are the words
that to my mouth rose willingly
like water at an overflowing rim;
yours the lone hours, when my expert lips
candidly moved forward for the kiss.

Taci, anima mia...

Taci, anima mia. Son questi i giorni
tetri che per inerzia si dura,
i giorni che nessuna attesa illude.
Come l'albero ignudo a mezzo inverno
che s'attedia nell'ombra della corte,
non m'aspetto di mettere più foglie
e dubito d'averle messe mai.

Nella folla che m'urta andando solo,
mi pare d'esser da me stesso assente.
E m'accalco ad udire dov'è ressa,
sosto dalle vetrine abbarbagliato
e mi volgo al frusciare d'ogni gonna.
Per la voce d'un cantastorie cieco
per l'improvviso lampo d'una nuca
mi sgocciolan dagli occhi sciocche lagrime
mi s'accendon negli occhi cupidigie.
Ché tutta la mia vita è nei miei occhi:
ogni cosa che passa la commuove
come debole vento un'acqua morta.
Non sono che uno specchio rassegnato.
In me stesso non guardo perché nulla
vi troverei...

E, venuta la sera, nel mio letto
mi stendo lungo come in una bara.

Softly, my soul . . .

Softly, my soul. These are the bleak
days we endure by sheer inertia,
days fooled by no expectation.
A barren tree halfway through winter,
lonely in the gloom of the backyard,
I think I'll never put out leaves and doubt
I ever did.

Crowds press against me as I walk.
I seem to be removed from my own self—
to rush where people gather,
to wander, dazed by windows,
and turn at the rustling of each skirt.
For a blind singer's voice
or the flash of a nape,
silly tears flood my cheeks,
lust flares in my watery eyes.

For all my soul is in my eyes:
anything flitting by makes it
ripple like weak wind stagnant water.
I'm nothing but a resigned mirror
and don't look at myself because I know
nothing's there to be found . . .
                    And I lie down,
when evening comes, as in my coffin.

Versi a Dina

I

La trama delle lucciole ricordi
sul mar di Nervi, mia dolcezza prima?
(trasognato paese dove fui
ieri e che già non riconosce il cuore).

Forse. Ma il gesto che ti incise dentro,
io non ricordo; e stillano in me dolce
parole che non sai d'aver dette.

Estrema delusione degli amanti!
invano mescolarono le vite
s'anche il bene superstite, i ricordi,
son mani che non giungono a toccarsi.

Ognuno resta con la sua perduta
felicità, un po' stupito e solo,
pel mondo vuoto di significato.
Miele segreto di che s'alimenta;
fin che sino il ricordo ne consuma
e tutto è come se non fosse stato.

Lines to Dina

I

Do you remember the fireflies' pattern
on the sea at Nervi,[1] my first love?
(Dreamland where I was yesterday and yet
the heart already does not recognize it.)

Maybe. But the gesture that engraved you
inside I don't remember; words you don't
know you uttered are dripping sweet in me.[2]

Ultimate disillusionment of lovers!
They joined their lives together to no use
if even the surviving good, their memories,
are hands that can't stretch out and touch.

Each remains with his lost happiness,
a bit astonished and alone,
in a meaningless world.
A hidden honey that nourishes him;
until even remembrance wastes us and
everything is as if it hadn't been.

---

[1] A town near Genoa
[2] *Sweet* stands for *sweetness* here.

Oh, come poca cosa quel che fu

da quello che non fu divide!

           Meno

che la scia della nave acqua da acqua.

Saranno state

le lucciole di Nervi, le cicale

e la casa sul mare di Loano,

e tutta la mia poca gioia—e tu—

fin che mi strazi questo ricordare.

How little parts what was from what was not!
Less than a ship's wake does water from water.

It must have been the fireflies at Nervi,
the cicadas, the home on Loano's sea,[3]
and my little joy—and you—until
this remembering rends me.

---

[3] Loano is another town near Genoa, by the Ligurian Sea.

DINO CAMPANA

Dino Campana was born in Marradi, near Faenza, in 1885. In 1906 he suffered a nervous breakdown and was confined to an asylum. His life was marked by mental illness, restlessness, and misfortune. He spent his earlier years studying, traveling the world (Europe, South America, Russia), and writing poetry, and he carried on a long and complicated love affair with the poet Sibilla Aleramo. In 1913 Campana gave the sole copy of his manuscript of his verses to the poets Papini and Soffici (editors of the literary journals *Lacerba* and *La voce* ["The Voice"]), and Soffici subsequently lost it. Although this experience was devastating, Campana managed to rewrite and publish his poems as *Canti orfici* ("Orphic Songs") in 1914. He volunteered for military service during World War I but was considered unfit to serve and in 1918 was committed to the mental hospital Castel Pulci, where he died of septic poisoning in 1932. The poems of *Canti orfici*, his only collection, express the poet's troubled relation with the world. Recurrent themes are death, melancholy, and alienation. Woman, in poems such as "La chimera" ("The Chimera") and "Giardino autunnale" ("Autumn Garden"), is often depicted as a mythical enchantress.

La chimera

Non so se tra rocce il tuo pallido
Viso m'apparve, o sorriso
Di lontananze ignote
Fosti, la china eburnea
Fronte fulgente o giovine
Suora de la Gioconda:
O delle primavere
Spente, per i tuoi mitici pallori
O Regina o Regina adolescente:
Ma per il tuo ignoto poema
Di voluttà e di dolore
Musica fanciulla esangue,
Segnato di linea di sangue
Nel cerchio delle labbra sinuose,
Regina de la melodia:
Ma per il vergine capo
Reclino, io poeta notturno
Vegliai le stelle vivide nei pelaghi del cielo,
Io per il tuo dolce mistero
Io per il tuo divenir taciturno.
Non so se la fiamma pallida
Fu dei capelli il vivente
Segno del suo pallore,
Non so se fu un dolce vapore,
Dolce sul mio dolore,

Chimera

I don't know if your pale face appeared
To me among rocks, or if you were
A smile of remote places,
Your bowed ivory brow
A glow, the Gioconda's young sister:
Or were you Queen, the adolescent queen
Of the dead springs for your mythical pallor:
But for your secret poem
Of sorrow and voluptuousness
Etched with a line of blood
In the sinuous lips' circle,
Musical bloodless girl,
You Queen of melody:
But for the virgin head
Recline, I, the night poet
contemplated the vivid
stars in seas of the sky,
I for your tender mystery
I for your taciturn becoming.
I do not know if the wan flame
of your hair was the living
brand of her pallor;
I do not know if it was a sweet vapor,
Sweet on my sorrow,

Sorriso di un volto notturno:

Guardo le bianche rocce le mute fonti dei venti

E l'immobilità dei firmamenti

E i gonfi rivi che vanno piangenti

E l'ombre del lavoro umano curve là sui poggi algenti

E ancora per teneri cieli lontane chiare ombre correnti

E ancora ti chiamo ti chiamo Chimera.

The smile of a nocturnal face:

I look at the white rocks the mute sources of winds

And the motionless firmaments

And swollen rivers that flow weeping

And the bent shadows

Of human toil there on the frigid hills

And still through gentle skies

The far clear running shadows

And I still keep on calling you Chimera.

Sogno di prigione

Nel viola della notte odo canzoni bronzee. La cella è bianca, il giaciglio è bianco. La cella è bianca, piena di un torrente di voci che muoiono nelle angeliche cune, delle voci angeliche bronzee è piena la cella bianca. Silenzio: il viola della notte: in rabeschi dalle sbarre bianche il blu del sonno. Penso ad Anika: stelle deserte sui monti nevosi: strade bianche deserte: poi chiese di marmo bianche: nelle strade Anika canta: un buffo dall'occhio infernale la guida, che grida. Ora il mio paese tra le montagne. Io al parapetto del cimitero davanti alla stazione che guardo il cammino nero delle macchine, su, giù. Non è ancor notte; silenzio occhiuto di fuoco: le macchine mangiano rimangiano il nero silenzio nel cammino della notte.

Un treno: si sgonfia arriva in silenzio, fermo: la porpora del treno morde la notte: dal parapetto del cimitero le occhiaie rosse che si gonfiano della notte: poi tutto, mi pare, si muta in rombo: *Da un finestrino in fuga io? io ch'alzo le braccia nella luce!!* (il treno mi passa sotto rombando come un demonio).

Jail Dream

In violet night I hear bronze songs. The cell is white, the pallet is white. The cell is white, filled with a stream of voices that die in the angelic cradles, the white cell is full of the angelic bronze voices. Silence: the night's purple: the night's blue in arabesques of white bars. I think of Anika: solitary stars on snowy mountains: white deserted streets: then white marble churches: in the streets Anika's singing: a hell-eyed clown leads her, screaming. Now my village in the mountains.[1] At the parapet of the cemetery in front of the station I, looking at the black flow of cars, up and down. It's not night yet; fiery-eyed silence: cars keep on eating black silence in the flow of night. A train: it lets off steam arrives in silence, it stops: the train's purple bites the night: from the cemetery's parapet red eye sockets are swelling in the night: then everything, it seems to me, turns into a roar: *Am I fleeing, at a window? is it I raising my arms into the light??* (the train goes under me, roaring like a devil).

---

[1] The village is the poet's native Marradi.

ARTURO ONOFRI

Arturo Onofri was born in Rome in 1885. He published *Liriche* ("Lyrics"), his first collection of poetry, in 1907 and cofounded the magazine *Lirica* ("Lyric Poetry") in 1912 and contributed poems and critical essays to *La voce*. He died in 1928. Traces of D'Annunzio, Pascoli, and Mallarmé can be found in his earlier verse. He was particularly gifted at writing lyrical fragments dedicated to the natural world. Topics include the seasons, the wind, and butterflies. Onofri was influenced by the philosopher Rudolf Steiner and in particular Steiner's doctrine of anthroposophy, a philosophy of the spirit. Religious motifs are frequent in Onofri's work, and many of the poems of *Poemi tragici* (1908; "Tragic Poems") and *Vincere il drago!* (1928; "Defeat the Dragon!") have spiritual themes, such as the celestial order of the cosmos, sacrifice, and redemption. He often employed analogy to forge new associations between the human and the divine.

Marzo

Marzo, che mette nuvole a soqquadro

e le ammontagna in alpi di broccati,

per poi disfarle in mammole sui prati,

accende all'improvviso, come un ladro,

un'occhiata di sole

che abbaglia acqua e viole.

Con in bocca un fil d'erba primaticcio,

Marzo è un fanciullo in ozio, a cavalcioni

sul vento che separa due stagioni;

e, zufolando, fa, per suo capriccio,

con strafottenti audacie,

il tempo che gli piace.

Stanotte, fra i suoi riccioli, spioventi

sul mio sonno a rovesci e a trilli alati,

il flauto di silenzio dei suoi fiati

vegetali svegliava azzurri e argenti

nel mio sognarlo, e fuori

ne son sbocciati i fiori.

March

March that dismembers clouds
and lifts them into mountains of brocade,
to later shred them—pansies in the meadows,
suddenly like a thief
        kindles a glance
          of sunshine in the waters.

A blade of grass between his teeth,
March is an idle kid, astride
the wind parting two seasons:
with brazen boldness he
        makes, just by whistling,
          the weather to his liking.

Last night, through his curls streaming
showers and chirpings on my sleep,
the mute flute of his vegetal
breath restored blues and silvers
        to my dreaming of him,
          and out sprang flowers.

The Lyrical Poets

Umberto Saba

Umberto Saba was born Umberto Poli in Trieste in 1883. His father abandoned the family before his birth, and Saba was raised by his mother according to the Jewish faith. He worked as a clerk and served briefly in the army, publishing his first collection of poetry, *Poesie* ("Poems"), in 1911. He spent most of his life in Trieste, where he opened an antiquarian shop, but was briefly forced to flee his native city to go into hiding when Mussolini enacted the racial laws. Saba continued writing poetry, much of which is collected in the volume *Canzoniere* ("Songbook"), which went through many editions, until his death in Gorizia in 1957. Trieste is a central figure in Saba's poetics, and in poems such as "Trieste" and "Città vecchia" ("Old City") the poet temporarily sublimates his suffering through communion with his city. Marginalization, illness, and grief are key themes in poems such as "Donna" ("Woman"), "La capra" ("The Goat"), and "Il poeta" ("The Poet"). Saba's clear and poignant lyrics commonly exalt humble and quotidian events or subjects, such as a cat or a stroll through the Jewish ghetto.

Donna

Quand'eri
giovinetta pungevi
come una mora di macchia. Anche il piede
t'era un'arma, o selvaggia.

Eri difficile a prendere.
        Ancora
giovane, ancora
sei bella. I segni
degli anni, quelli del dolore, legano
l'anime nostre, una ne fanno. E dietro
i capelli nerissimi che avvolgo
alle mie dita, più non temo il piccolo
bianco puntuto orecchio demoniaco.

Woman

When you were young
you pricked like a wood berry.
Even your foot was a weapon, you wild one.

You played hard to get.
    And now,
still young,
you're beautiful as then.
The marks of time, of pain, link our souls
making them one. Beneath the raven hair
I wind around my fingers, I
no longer fear
your tiny, white, devilish pointed ear.

Teatro degli Artigianelli

Falce e martello e la stella d'Italia
ornano nuovi la sala. Ma quanto
dolore per quel segno su quel muro!

Entra, sorretto dalle grucce, il Prologo.
Saluta al pugno, dice sue parole
perché le donne ridano e i fanciulli
che affollano la povera platea.
Dice, timido ancora, dell'idea
che gli animi affratella; chiude: «E adesso
faccio come i tedeschi: mi ritiro.»
Tra un atto e l'altro, alla Cantina, in giro
rosseggia parco ai bicchieri l'amico
dell'uomo, cui rimargina ferite,
gli chiude solchi dolorosi; alcuno
venuto qui da spaventosi esigli,
si scalda a lui come chi ha freddo al sole.

Questo è il Teatro degli Artigianelli,
quale lo vide il poeta nel mille
novecentoquarantaquattro, un giorno
di Settembre, che a tratti
rombava ancora il cannone, e Firenze
taceva, assorta nelle sue rovine.

Arts and Crafts Theater

Hammer and sickle and the star of Italy
now decorate the Hall.[1]
How much pain
for that banner on the wall!

Leaning on crutches, the M.C. walks in,
salutes the audience with his fist,
cracks jokes to get women and boys
crowding the stalls to laugh.
Still timidly, he mentions the idea
that makes men brothers, then: "And now I'll do
what the krauts always do: beat a retreat!"
Between acts, in the cellar,
sparkles man's sober friend in glasses—
healing old sorrows, cauterizing wounds.
Some who came here from exile
warm themselves at its flame
like numbed men in the sun.

This is the Arts and Crafts Theater as the poet
saw it in nineteen-hundred-forty-four:
it was September, the guns rumbled sparsely,
Florence was quietly brooding on her ruins.

---

[1] The symbol used by Communists in their flag. Here Saba is misinformed, because
the flag he depicts, with the stars, was the Soviet one. The poem remains, nonetheless,
an epic one in its celebration of freedom.

VINCENZO CARDARELLI

Vincenzo Cardarelli was born Nazzareno Caldarelli in Corneto Tarquinia, near Viterbo, in 1887. For the most part self-educated, Cardarelli moved to Rome when he was nineteen and supported himself through a variety of odd jobs. From 1909 to 1912 he was romantically involved with the poet Sibilla Aleramo. In 1911 he published his first poems in literary journals including *La voce* and *Lirica* ("Lyric Poetry"), and in 1916 his first complete collection, *Prologhi* ("Prologues"), appeared. In 1919 he cofounded *La ronda*, a literary review that called for a return to Leopardi's lyricism. In 1942 Cardarelli's collected poems were published as *Poesie* ("Poems"). He spent most of his life in Rome, where he directed *La fiera letteraria* ("The Literary Fair") until his death in 1959. Often described as a morally rigid poet, he promoted a return to classicism, away from any literary decadence. The passing of time (days, seasons, years) is a central trope in his work, and several poems center on the cycle of life.

Saluto di stagione

Benvenuta estate.

Alla tua decisa maturità

m'affido.

Mi poserò ai tuoi soli,

ricambierò alla terra

in tanto sudore caldo

delle mie adempiute nutrizioni

i suoi veleni vitali.

Lascio la primavera

dietro di me

come un amore insano

d'adolescente.

Lascio i languori e le ottusità,

i sonni impossibili,

le faticose inerzie animali,

il tempo neutro e vuoto

in cui l'uomo è stagione.

Io che amo i tempi fermi e le superfici chiare,

e ad ogni transizione di meriggio

sento il limite e il male

che incrinano ogni cambio d'ora,

saluto nel sole d'estate

la forza dei giorni più eguali.

Season's Greetings

Welcome, summer. I trust
in your steadfast maturity.
I will live by your fire,
returning to the earth
in so much perspiration
vital poisons that fed me.

I leave springtime behind,
youngsters' infatuations.
I leave languor and bluntness,
insomnia, body inertia,
the amorphous stint when man
is only season.

I who cherish firm weather
and neat surfaces, and
at each high-noon commotion
feel the prison and evil
that chip each change of hour,
greet in the July sun
the force of calmer days.

Estiva

Distesa estate,

stagione dei densi climi

dei grandi mattini

dell'albe senza rumore—

ci si risveglia come in un acquario—

dei giorni identici, astrali,

stagione la meno dolente

d'oscuramenti e di crisi,

felicità degli spazi,

nessuna promessa terrena

può dare pace al mio cuore

quanto la certezza di sole

che dal tuo cielo trabocca,

stagione estrema, che cadi

prostrata in riposi enormi,

dai oro ai più vasti sogni,

stagione che porti la luce

a distendere il tempo

di là dai confini del giorno,

e sembri mettere a volte

nell'ordine che procede

qualche cadenza dell'indugio eterno.

Summer Song

Placated summer, season
of palpable climates, huge mornings,
noiseless dawns. One awakens
in an aquarium—starry,
similar days least hitting
with darkenings and crises.
Buoyancy of space.

No earthly promise
can give peace to my heart
like this certainty of sun
cascading from the sky,
season of extremes falling
dead tired in deep slumber,
gilding the highest dreams,

season that brings us light
to extend the hour
beyond the boundaries of day
and seems to put at times
in the order that proceeds
a cadence of the godly pause.

GIUSEPPE UNGARETTI

Giuseppe Ungaretti was born in Alexandria, Egypt, in 1888 to Italian parents. He traveled to Paris in 1912, where he participated in the city's lively cosmopolitan culture and socialized with many members of the Parisian avant-garde (including Picasso and Apollinaire). In 1914 he earned a degree in letters from the Sorbonne. While serving in the Italian army's nineteenth regiment during World War I, Ungaretti wrote some of his best-known poems, which are collected in *Il porto sepolto* (1916; "The Buried Harbor"). His war experiences resulted in a spiritual crisis during the 1920s. In 1936 financial hardship forced him to take a teaching post in São Paulo, Brazil. In 1939 his son Antonietto died following a botched operation, a great blow to the poet. Ungaretti's collections are *Allegria di naufragi* (1919; "The Joy of Shipwrecks"), *Sentimento del tempo* (1933; "The Feeling of Time"), and *Il dolore* (1947; "Pain"). He died in Milan in 1970. Although originally enthusiastic about Italy's intervention in the war, he experienced a transformation of perspective after witnessing death firsthand. His wartime poetry, such as "Fratelli" ("Brothers") and "Veglia" ("Keeping Vigil"), is interested in issues of disanimation and detachment. Nostalgia, grief, and memory are frequent themes in his lyrical poems, many of which are written as fragments.

Fratelli

Di che reggimento siete
fratelli?

Parola tremante
nella notte

Foglia appena nata

Nell'aria spasimante
involontaria rivolta
dell'uomo presente alla sua
fragilità

Fratelli

Mariano il 15 luglio 1916

Brothers

What's your regiment,
brothers?

Word wavering
in the night

Unfurling leaf

In the anguished air
primal rebellion
of man
facing his frailty

Brothers

Mariano, 15 July 1916

Veglia

Un'intera nottata

buttato vicino

a un compagno

massacrato

con la sua bocca

digrignata

volta al plenilunio

con la congestione

delle sue mani

penetrata

nel mio silenzio

ho scritto

lettere piene d'amore

Non sono mai stato

tanto

attaccato alla vita

Altitudine 4, 23 dicembre 1915

Keeping Vigil

A whole night
lying by
a slaughtered
friend
his twisted
mouth
turned to the full moon
his bloated
hands
invading
my silence
I wrote
letters filled with love

Never have I been
so attached
to life

Altitude 4, 23 December 1915

C'era una volta

Bosco Cappuccio

ha un declivio

di velluto verde

come una dolce

poltrona

Appisolarmi là

solo

in un caffé remoto

con una luce fievole

come questa

di questa luna

Quota Centoquarantuno l'1 agosto 1916

Once upon a Time

Cappuccio Wood
has a green
velvet slope
like a soft
armchair

To snooze up there
alone in a cafe
off the beaten track
with a glimmer
faint like this
from this moon

Altitude 141, 1 August 1916

Sono una creatura

Come questa pietra
del S. Michele
così fredda
così dura
così prosciugata
così refrattaria
così totalmente
disanimata

Come questa pietra
è il mio pianto
che non si vede

La morte
si sconta
vivendo

Valloncello di Cima Quattro il 5 agosto 1916

I Am a Presence

Like this stone
of Mount Michael
so cold
so hard
so dried up
so fireproof
so totally
soulless

Like this stone's core
are my tears—
they can't be seen

We pay
for death
by living

Altitude 4, 5 August 1916

San Martino del Carso

Di queste case

non è rimasto

che qualche

brandello di muro

Di tanti che mi corrispondevano

non è rimasto

neppure tanto

Ma nel cuore

nessuna croce manca

È il mio cuore

il paese più straziato

Valloncello dell'Albero Isolato il 27 agosto 1916

San Martino del Carso

Nothing has remained
of these houses
but some chunks
of plaster

Of so many
who cared for me
not even that much
has remained

But in my heart
I keep every cross

My heart
is the most torn land

Mound of the Lonely Tree, 27 August 1916

Nostalgia

Quando
la notte è a svanire
poco prima di primavera
e di rado
qualcuno passa

Su Parigi s'addensa
un oscuro colore
di pianto

In un canto
di ponte
contemplo
l'illimitato silenzio
di una ragazza
tenue

Le nostre
malattie
si fondono

E come portati via
si rimane

Locovizza il 28 settembre 1916

Nostalgia

When night
draws to a close
just before spring
and very few
people go by

a dark color
of weeping
covers Paris

By the railing
on a bridge
I watch
the boundless silence
of a thin
girl

Our maleurs
become
one

And it's like being
carried away

Locovizza, 28 September 1916

EUGENIO MONTALE

Eugenio Montale was born in Genoa in 1896 and spent much of his early life on the Ligurian Riviera. He began writing poems at an early age, publishing his first collection, *Ossi di seppia* ("Cuttlefish Bones"), in 1925. Although Montale took part in World War I as an infantryman, he later refused to join the Fascist Party, an ethical position that resulted in the loss of his post as director of the Vieusseux Library in Florence in 1938. He moved to Milan to become a critic for the newspaper *Corriere della sera* ("Evening Courier"). Montale's major poetry collections are *Le occasioni* (1939; "The Occasions"), *La bufera ed altro* (1956; "'The Storm' and Other Poems"), and *Satura* (1971). He won countless literary prizes, including the Nobel Prize for Literature in 1975. He is one of six Italians to have received this honor. He died in Milan in 1981. A dialectics of negativity is omnipresent in his poetry (clear in "I limoni" ["The Lemons"]), which is marked by a dissonant relation with the world. In Montale's poetry, unlike that of D'Annunzio, doubt and uncertainty prevail over empirical truth. Montale is far from nihilistic, however, as humble or marginal living things or objects (eels, broken bottles) flourish in the most barren of landscapes.

Valmorbia

Valmorbia, discorrevano il tuo fondo
fioriti nuvoli di piante agli àsoli.
Nasceva in noi, volti dal cieco caso,
oblio del mondo.

Tacevano gli spari, nel grembo solitario
non dava suono che il Leno roco.
Sbocciava un razzo su lo stelo, fioco
lacrimava nell'aria.

Le notti chiare erano tutte un'alba
e portavano volpi alla mia grotta.
Valmorbia, un nome—e ora nella scialba
memoria, terra dove non annotta.

Valmorbia

The breezes drove burgeoning puffs of plants
all rustling through your valley.
Oblivion of the world was born in us,
driven into blind alleys.

The guns were silent, in your lonely womb
only the Leno's harsh flow would you hear.
A rocket bloomed on its stem
then dimly came down like a tear.

Clear nights were just like dawn
and led foxes to my lair.
Valmorbia—a name: now in my waning memory
a land where light ever stares.

Portami il girasole...

Portami il girasole ch'io lo trapianti

nel mio terreno bruciato dal salino,

e mostri tutto il giorno agli azzurri specchianti

del cielo l'ansietà del suo volto giallino.

Tendono alla chiarità le cose oscure,

si esauriscono i corpi in un fluire

di tinte: queste in musiche. Svanire

è dunque la ventura delle venture.

Portami tu la pianta che conduce

dove sorgono bionde trasparenze

e vapora la vita quale essenza;

portami il girasole impazzito di luce.

Bring me the sunflower . . .

Bring me the sunflower that I may plant it
in the garden patch burned by sea salt:
it will show to the mirroring blues
its anxious yellow face all day.

Dark things have a yearning for clarity,
bodies dissolve, a flow
of hues, these to music. So
to melt is the best of happenings.

Bring me the plant that leads to
where gold transparencies rise
and life distills like essence:
bring me the sunflower crazed with light.

Meriggiare pallido e assorto...

Meriggiare pallido e assorto
presso un rovente muro d'orto,
ascoltare tra i pruni e gli sterpi
schiocchi di merli, frusci di serpi.

Nelle crepe del suolo o su la veccia
spiar le file di rosse formiche
ch'ora si rompono ed ora s'intrecciano
a sommo di minuscole biche.

Osservare tra frondi il palpitare
lontano di scaglie di mare
mentre si levano tremuli scricchi
di cicale dai calvi picchi.

E andando nel sole che abbaglia
sentire con triste meraviglia
com'è tutta la vita e il suo travaglio
in questo seguitare una muraglia
che ha in cima cocci aguzzi di bottiglia.

Pensive and pale, to spend . . .

Pensive and pale, to spend the afternoon
by a sun-roasted garden wall,
to listen in the thorny undergrowth
to snakes that slither and blackbirds that call.

On vetch, on the cracked ground
to spot ranks of red ants
breaking and intermingling
on top of tiny mounds.

To watch through branches the
far sea shining like blades
while cicadas raise quivering
creaks from the barren peaks.

And, going in the glaring sun,
wonder at the sadness of it all:
how all our struggles come to
a jagged, glass-capped wall.

L'altro

Non so chi se n'accorga

ma i nostri commerci con l'Altro

furono un lungo inghippo. Denunziarli

sarà, più che un atto d'ossequio, un impetrare clemenza.

Non siamo responsabili di non essere lui

né ha colpa lui, o merito, della nostra parvenza.

Non c'è neppure timore. Astuto il flamengo nasconde

il capo sotto l'ala e crede che il cacciatore

non lo veda.

The Other

I don't know if anyone sees it
but our dealings with the Other
were a big mess. To account for them
will be, more than fawning, begging for mercy.
We're not responsible for not being him
nor is he guilty, or proud of our appearance.
There's no fear, even. The astute flamingo
hides head under wing and thinks
the hunter does not see it.

Avrei voluto sentirmi...

Avrei voluto sentirmi scabro ed essenziale

siccome i ciottoli che tu volvi,

mangiati dalla salsedine;

scheggia fuori del tempo, testimone

di una volontà fredda che non passa.

Altro fui: uomo intento che riguarda

in sé, in altrui, il bollore

della vita fugace—uomo che tarda

all'atto, che nessuno, poi, distrugge.

Volli cercare il male

che tarla il mondo, la piccola stortura

d'una leva che arresta

l'ordegno universale; e tutti vidi

gli eventi del minuto

come pronti a disgiungersi in un crollo.

Seguìto il solco d'un sentiero m'ebbi

l'opposto in cuore, col suo invito; e forse

m'occorreva il coltello che recide,

la mente che decide e si determina.

Altri libri occorrevano

a me, non la tua pagina rombante.

Ma nulla so rimpiangere: tu sciogli

ancora i groppi interni col tuo canto.

Il tuo delirio sale agli astri ormai.

I would have liked to feel . . .

I would have liked to feel scoured, bared
like the pebbles you roll,
eaten away by salt;
a splinter out of time, a witness to
a cold, everlasting will.
Instead I was a man bent on watching
in himself and others the stew
of fleeting life: a man slow to actions
that later no one destroys.
I would have liked to find the evil
rotting the world, the puny lever's flaw
that blocks the universal clock.
And I saw all the events of the present
as if about to fall apart and downcrash.
Having followed one path, my heart
chose the opposite, tempted:
perhaps I needed a sharper knife,
a mind that decides then stays put.
Other books I needed, not your seething page.
But there is nothing I regret: you still
smoothe my inner roughness with your song.
Your frenzy already is soaring to the stars.

Ho sostato talvolta...

Ho sostato talvolta nelle grotte

che t'assecondano, vaste

o anguste, ombrose e amare.

Guardati dal fondo gli sbocchi

segnavano architetture

possenti campite di cielo.

Sorgevano dal tuo petto

rombante aerei templi,

guglie scoccanti luci;

una città di vetro dentro l'azzurro netto

via via si discopriva da ogni caduco velo

e il suo rombo non era che un susurro.

Nasceva dal fiotto la patria sognata.

Dal subbuglio emergeva l'evidenza.

L'esiliato rientrava nel paese incorrotto.

Così, padre, dal tuo disfrenamento

si afferma, chi ti guardi, una legge severa.

Ed è vano sfuggirla: mi condanna

s'io lo tento anche un ciottolo

róso sul mio cammino,

impietrato soffrire senza nome,

o l'informe rottame

che gittò fuor del corso la fiumara

del vivere in un fitto di ramure e di strame.

I have sometimes paused . . .

I have sometimes paused in the grottoes

that you mold vast or narrow, dark and bitter.

Seen from below, the exits

marked powerful architectures

etched on the sky.

From your roaring chest airy temples

arose, spires shooting light.

Bit by bit then a crystal city—

inside the stark blue—shed

every ephemeral veil,

and its rumble was only a whisper.

The longed-for motherland bloomed from the foam.

From the turmoil, proof at last emerged.

The exile returned to his innocent town.

So, if one observes you, father,

your wildness displays a stern law:

to flee from it is useless; if I try,

even a worn stone on my path condemns me

with its fixed, nameless pain, or the shapeless

refuse the stream of life

threw out of its bed into a thicket of branches and dung.

Nel destino che si prepara

c'è forse per me sosta,

niun'altra minaccia.

Questo ripete il flutto in sua furia incomposta,

e questo ridice il filo della bonaccia.

In the destiny that awaits me

perhaps I will find a lull—

certainly no more threats.

This the surf states in its unquiet fury,

and this repeats the zephyr of good weather.

Scirocco

O rabido ventare di scirocco
che l'arsiccio terreno gialloverde
bruci;
e su nel cielo pieno
di smorte luci
trapassa qualche biocco
di nuvola, e si perde.
Ore perplesse, brividi
d'una vita che fugge
come acqua tra le dita;
inafferrati eventi,
luci—ombre, commovimenti
delle cose malferme della terra;
oh alide ali dell'aria
ora son io
l'agave che s'abbarbica al crepaccio
dello scoglio
e sfugge al mare da le braccia d'alghe
che spalanca ampie gole e abbranca rocce;
e nel fermento
d'ogni essenza, coi miei racchiusi bocci
che non sanno più esplodere oggi sento
la mia immobilità come un tormento.

Scirocco

Raging scirocco wind,

you who scorch the parched

yellow-green ground

while up in the sky

streaked with wan fires

rare flaky clouds go by . . .

Distracted hours, tremors

of a life trickling

like water through our fingers;

misunderstood occurrences,

shadows and lights, commotion

of earthly, unsteady things—

O withered wings of air,

now I'm the agave clinging

to a crevice in the reef, fleeing

the alga-tentacled sea

that opens gasping chasms and grabs rocks;

now in the tumult of each essence

my buds, no longer able to burst forth,

writhe in their immobility.

Maria Luisa Spaziani

The poet, novelist, playwright, and critic Maria Luisa Spaziani was born in 1924 in Turin, where she completed her studies with a dissertation on Proust. In 1949 she met the poet Eugenio Montale, and so began a lifelong friendship based on their mutual interest in poetry and music. In 1950 Spaziani won the Premio Viareggio for journalism. Her earliest collection of poetry, *Le acque del Sabato* ("The Waters of the Sabbath"), was published in 1954. Her other major publications are *Utilità della memoria* (1966; "The Usefulness of Memory") and *La stella del libero arbitrio* (1986; "The Star of Free Will"). Spaziani spent much of her life alone, living in Milan, Rome, and later Messina, Sicily, where she taught French literature. She won many literary prizes for her work (which was translated into many languages) and was often nominated as Italy's candidate for the Nobel Prize for Literature. Although often labeled hermetic, her poetry is not easily categorized. In poems such as "Inutilità della memoria" ("The Futility of Memory"), poetry is potentially curative, while memory and commemoration are key themes in poems such as "Alle vittime di Mauthausen" ("To the Victims of Mauthausen").

Il destino

Fu allora che il destino mi volle prendere per mano;
da questo istante, disse, la tua bianca esistenza
in me si fonde, assume una forma mai vista—
da questo istante intuisci l'infinito dei cieli.

Decifrare dei rebus è stata la tua vita:
eccoti ora la chiave, un solo sole t'illumina,
guarda di che colore si sono fatti i fiori
quando alle tue pupille ho detto *apritevi*—

La morte è un radicale mozzafiato
ma ti è dato di scorgere il rovescio della medaglia—
ti hanno detto, bambina, che Dio è in ogni cosa
ed era un puro apologo, sinonimo di poesia.

Sei stata imprigionata in un castello di nebbie
con la mente allo stadio di pipistrello cieco—
ora cammina, alzati, ti dico. Prima di te l'ho detto
a Euridice, a Lazzaro, a ogni primavera stregata.

Destiny

It was then that destiny decided to take me by the hand:
from this moment on, destiny said, your empty existence
will melt into me, take on a form never seen;
from this moment on, you will intuit the immensity of the skies.

Decoding puzzles has been your life;
here now is the key, one sun illuminates you,
look at the color the flowers have turned
since I said simply to your eyes *open wide.*

Death really knocks the wind out of you,
but it is given to you to unveil the other side of the coin—
they told you when you were a little girl, that God is everywhere,
but it was pure apologue, a synonym for poetry.

You've been locked in a castle of fogs,
your mind at the blind-bat stage—
now walk, arise, I say to you. Before you, I said it
to Eurydice, to Lazarus, to every bewitched springtime.

Il Duomo

Quando stavo a Milano il Duomo aveva trent'anni di meno,
valchiria folle marzo galoppava,
un cielo di struggente acquamarina
mi rideva in pupille di pochi ricordi.

Ragazzetta la quercia del collegio
stringevano sul cuore trenta cerchi di meno,
la torre Velasca brillava nuova di zecca
riflettendo tramonti da isole papuasiche.

Come un cero la linguetta di fuoco,
ogni guglia scalare reggeva il suo santo.
Li vedo sorridere, con la mia vista d'aquila,
palpebrare e ripetermi di sì.

Sotto tre lune piene ruotanti tutte insieme
per me fioriva fitto sul sagrato
un prato di narcisi su cui danzava Rimbaud.
Avevo qualche aureola in più, nel marzo di Milano.

The Duomo

When I lived in Milan the Duomo was thirty years younger,
March used to gallop along like a crazed Valkyrie,
a sky of thawing aquamarine
used to laugh into my eyes remembering little.

When I was a girl, the schoolyard oak
held thirty circles fewer to its heart,
the Velasca tower shined sparkling new,
reflecting Papuan island sunsets.

As a candle holds its wick of flame,
each craggy spire held its saint.
With my eagle eye I saw them smile,
wink, and repeat to me yes.

Beneath three full moons in joint rotation
there bloomed for me, thick on the churchyard pavement,
a field of narcissus where Rimbaud danced.
I had a halo or two more then, that March in Milan.

Antonia Pozzi

Antonia Pozzi was born in 1912 in Milan into an upper-class family. She spent much of her time in her room and kept her poetry to herself. The love of her life was her Latin teacher, Antonio Cervi. Her parents did not approve of the match (Cervi was not her social equal) and forbade the marriage. She studied philology at the University of Milan and later found a teaching post. The imminent war and the passing of the racial laws in 1938 led to a gradual deterioration of her health and humor. In December 1938 she was found frozen in the city suburbs after having taken an overdose of pills. A selection of her poetry was published posthumously by her father in the collection *Parole* (1939; "Words"), and poems were added in subsequent editions. Pozzi was keenly interested in the passing of time and the past-present continuum. Nostalgia, maternity, and the seasons are frequent themes in her work. For her, poetry has a redemptive function (e.g., "Preghiera alla poesia" ["Prayer to Poetry"]).

La porta che si chiude

Tu lo vedi, sorella: io sono stanca—
come il pilastro d'un cancello angusto
diga nel tempo all'irruente fuga
d'una folla rinchiusa.

Oh, le parole prigioniere
che battono battono
furiosamente
alla porta dell'anima
e la porta dell'anima
che a palmo a palmo
spietatamente
si chiude!

Ed ogni giorno il varco si stringe
ed ogni giorno l'assalto è più duro.

E l'ultimo giorno—
io lo so—
l'ultimo giorno,
quando un'unica lama di luce
pioverà dall'estremo spiraglio
dentro la tenebra,
allora sarà l'urto tremendo,
l'urlo mortale

The Closing Door

As you see, sister, I am tired—
like the post of a narrow gate
dam against the erupting flight
of a pent-up mob.

Oh, imprisoned words
that are pounding, pounding
furiously
at the door of the soul
and the door of the soul
that inch by inch
is pitilessly
closing!

And every day the exit narrows
and every day the attack is fiercer.

And on the last day—
I know it—
on the last day,
when a single blade of light
falls from the farthest opening
in the darkness,
the clash will be tremendous,
the mortal scream

delle parole non nate
verso l'ultimo sogno di sole.

E poi,
dietro la porta per sempre chiusa,
sarà la notte intera,
la frescura,
il silenzio.

E poi, con le labbra serrate,
con gli occhi aperti
sull'arcano cielo dell'ombra,
sarà
—tu lo sai—
la pace.

of unborn words

toward the final dream of sunlight.

And then,

behind the door forever closed,

there will be total night,

cool air,

silence.

And then, with tight lips,

with eyes open

to the shadow's eerie sky,

will be

—you know it—

peace.

Presagio

Esita l'ultima luce
fra le dita congiunte dei pioppi—
l'ombra trema di freddo e d'attesa
dietro di noi
e lenta muove intorno le braccia
per farci più soli.

Cade l'ultima luce
sulle chiome dei tigli—
in cielo le dita dei pioppi
s'inanellano di stelle.

Qualcosa dal cielo discende
verso l'ombra che trema—
qualcosa passa
nella tenebra nostra
come un biancore—
forse qualcosa che ancora non è—
forse qualcuno che sarà
domani—
forse una creatura del nostro pianto.

Premonition

The last light lingers
between the poplars' joined fingers—
the shadow trembles with cold and expectancy
behind us
and slowly turns its arms around
to make us more lonely.

The last light falls
on the lindens' manes—
in the sky the fingers of the poplars
put on their rings of stars.

Something descends from high
toward the trembling shadow—
something goes by
in our darkness
like a whiteness—
perhaps something that does not exist yet—
perhaps someone
who will exist tomorrow—
perhaps a creature of our weeping.

The Hermeticists

SALVATORE QUASIMODO

The 1959 Nobel Prize laureate Salvatore Quasimodo was born in Modica, Sicily, in 1901 into a working-class family. He studied to be an engineer and worked for some time as a surveyor. In 1928 he turned to writing and published his first collection of poems, *Acque e terre* ("Water and Land"), in 1929 in the journal *Solaria*. In 1941 he accepted the chair of Italian literature in Milan. He traveled all over the world. He died in Naples in 1968 of a cerebral hemorrhage. Quasimodo's poetry can be divided into two categories, separated by the experience of World War II. His prewar and war poetry, in collections such as *Poesie* (1938; "Poems"), *Lirici greci* (1940; "Greek Lyrical Poets"), and *Ed è subito sera* (1942; "And Suddenly It's Evening"), is decidedly hermetic and frequently deals with his native Sicily. In 1945, after the devastation that Italy underwent as a result of Fascism and the Nazi occupation, Quasimodo declared the hermetic movement over and went on to write politically and socially engaged lyrics. *Giorno dopo giorno* (1947; "Day after Day"), for example, chronicles the lack of humanity during the war and was held up as a handbook of the new left in Italy.

Alle fronde dei salici

E come potevamo noi cantare
con il piede straniero sopra il cuore,
fra i morti abbandonati nelle piazze
sull'erba dura di ghiaccio, al lamento
della madre che andava incontro al figlio
crocifisso al palo del telegrafo?
Alle fronde dei salici, per voto,
anche le nostre cetre erano appese,
oscillavano lievi al triste vento.

To the Willow Branches

How could we sing,
a foreign boot crushing our hearts,[1]
among the dead left in the squares
on the hard frozen grass, to bleating cries
of children, to the funereal howl
of mother meeting her son crucified
on a telegraph pole?
As a vow, even our zithers hung
from willow branches: and they swung
lightly in the bitter wind.

---

[1] The boot refers to the Nazi occupation of Milan after 25 July 1943.

Ancora dell' inferno

Non ci direte una notte gridando
dai megafoni, una notte
di zagare di nascite, d'amori
appena cominciati, che l'idrogeno
in nome del diritto brucia
la terra. Gli animali i boschi fondono
nell'Arca della distruzione, il fuoco
è un vischio sui crani dei cavalli,
negli occhi umani. Poi a noi morti
voi morti direte nuove tavole
della legge. Nell'antico linguaggio,
altri segni, profili di pugnali.

Balbetterà qualcuno sulle scorie,
inventerà tutto ancora
o nulla nella sorte uniforme,
il mormorio delle correnti, il crepitare
della luce. Non la speranza
direte voi morti alla nostra morte,
negli imbuti di fanghiglia bollente,
qui nell'inferno.

Still of Hell

You will not tell us one night bawling
from the loudspeakers, a night of orange blossoms
and births, of just begun loves: hydrogen
in the name of right is burning the earth.
Animals and woods melt in the Ark
of destruction, fire is lime
on horses' skulls, in human eyes.
Then to us dead you dead
will spell new tablets of the law.
In the old language, other
signs and outlines of knives.
Someone will babble on debris,
conjure up everything again
or nothing in the common lot—
murmur of streams, shimmer of light.
You dead won't say
hope to our death in pits
of boiling mud, here in hell.

SANDRO PENNA

Sandro Penna was born in Perugia in 1906. Greatly influenced by Leopardi, Penna's earlier poetry details the irreconcilable schism between the self and the natural world. After his father kicked him out of his house as a result of many disagreements (among them, Penna's career ambitions and his homosexuality), Penna moved to Rome and continued to write poems, which he sent to Saba, who reviewed them with enthusiasm. He published his first collection, *Poesie* ("Poems"), in 1939, followed by *Appunti* (1950; "Notes") and *Una strana gioia di vivere* (1956; "A Strange Joy of Living"). He continued writing and publishing his poetry until his death in Rome in 1977. His poems are for the most part short, many in the form of epigrams, and are written in a direct and evocative language. Much of his erotic poetry details homosexual love, particularly the attraction to young boys, and the poet exalts various characters that he has come into contact with (e.g., soldiers, errand boys, cyclists, and sailors). Memory is also important in Penna's poetics, and many poems are attempts to memorialize experiences long past.

Fanciullo, non fuggire,...

Fanciullo, non fuggire, non andare
solo. Non è per me che lo dico.
Io ti ho visto alla fronte un segno chiaro.
E tua madre non vede. Non vede l'amico.

Salgono in compagnia...

Salgono in compagnia dei genitori
i bei ragazzi dagli occhi legati.
Noi siamo qui, senza malinconia,
avidi un poco, poveri soldati.

È l'ora in cui si baciano...

È l'ora in cui si baciano i marmocchi
assonnati sui caldi ginocchi.
Ma io, per lunghe strade, coi miei occhi
inutilmente. Io, mostro da niente.

Boy, don't go alone, . . .

Boy, don't go alone, don't run away.
I don't say this just for my sake.
On your forehead I saw a plain sign.
Both your mother and your friend are blind.

The lovely boys, . . .

The lovely boys, eyes straight ahead,
saunter out by their parents led.
A trifle envious, we cannot stray far—
but no complaints, poor soldiers that we are.

This is the hour when kids . . .

This is the hour when kids are kissed,
sleepy on warm knees. But I,
on wearying streets, my eyes
no use to me, a monster to be hissed at.

MARIO LUZI

The poet, playwright, novelist, and critic Mario Luzi was born in Castello, a small town outside Florence, in 1914. He published his first collection of poetry, *La barca* ("The Boat"), considered the manifesto for the hermetic movement, in 1935. After taking a degree in French literature in 1936 at the University of Florence, he was active in the intellectual culture of Italy, collaborating on journals such as *Frontespizio* ("Frontispiece") and *Letteratura* ("Literature") and socializing with poets like Montale and Attilio Bertolucci. Since 1955 Luzi has taught French literature at the University of Florence. An avid traveler, he went to Russia, India, and the United States. His poems have been translated into more than a dozen languages. His earlier works, such as *Avvento notturno* (1938; "Nocturnal Advent") and *Quaderno Gotico* (1947; "Gothic Notebook"), are decidedly hermetic and contain religious motifs such as suffering and redemption. He is a Catholic. Later collections—*Onore del vero* (1957; "Honor of Truth"), *Nel magma* (1963; "In the Magma"), and *Libro di Ipazia* (1978; "Book of Ipazia")—are more ironic and ethical in nature and have moved away from a nostalgic tone.

Pur che...

Che nascita, che morte, che stagioni,
ombra che sei, tritata a questa mola,
pur che un vetro si turbi, una speranza
di fiori brilli e trepidi sui vasi.

Nascita e morte, verità veloce...
Si è qui, come si deve, in una parte,
in un punto del tempo, in una stanza,
nella luce, nel divenire eterno.

Altra sorte non so che non sia questa,
siedo rapito in questa fiamma fine,
guardo la chiara lamina febbrile
del giorno, mentre in cielo è già inverno.

Versi dal monte

Il primo vento miete nella selva.
Che fai? ti spero salda al proprio ramo...
appena ieri, appena ieri, mormoro.
Ora il pensiero a stento tiene uniti
e stretti in cerchio attorno al mite fuoco
gli idoli nella sua dolce caverna.

If Only . . .

What birth, what death, what seasons,
shadow that you are, ground under this mill,
if only a pane be rattled, a hope
of flowers shine and quiver on your sill!

Birth and death, a truth racing . . .
We are here, as we must be, in a place,
somewhere in time, in a room,
in the light, in the unceasing moving.

This is the life I've got to live.
I sit entranced by a fine flame,
looking at the feverish, sharp blade
of day as winter falls over the sky.

Lines from the Mountainside

The first wind is reaping in the woods.
What are you doing? Clinging,
I hope, to your green branch . . .
Just yesterday, just yesterday, I murmur.
Now thought in its sweet cave
can hardly hold together
the idols huddled tight by the weak flame.

Poscritto

Oppure quando a mezzo mattino, in una secca della
        ininterrotta disputa
un raptus di solitudine si sfrena
e «che vorresti veramente dire, voce umana?» s'insinua
quasi dentro una ridotta dell'anima, e lavora, un pensiero corvino.

«Sì, le tue cadenze secolari, i tuoi più casuali
e sbadati intercalari uditi ripetersi,
inseguire se stessi con un tonfo sommesso di tamburo
        sotterraneo—
ma il seme irraggiungibile, il mai bene il mai tutto
        affiorato del messaggio...»

Non so di nessuna chirurgia del cuore
che possa metterlo a nudo, decifrarne il senso—mi dico:
la grazia, forse (penso spesso a lei,
non me ne viene molta pace) ma troppo raramente
anch'essa e istantanea, nel controluce di un lampo.

Senonché il fuoco è presente, e questo è già tutto.

Postscript

When in the middle of the morning, in a lull
in the tireless argument
a surge of loneliness tears itself free
and: "Human voice,
what would you really like to say?"
darkly insinuates itself
into a cranny of the soul, gnawing away.

"Yes, your worldly phrases, your most
casual and worn-out talks echoing,
pursuing each other to the muffled
beat of a subterranean drum—
but the unreachable seed, the never stark
never total emerging of the word . . ."

I know no surgery of the heart that can
lay it bare, unscramble its meaning.
Grace perhaps (I often think of it—
not much peace in that), but it, too, rare
and instant as a bolt of lightning.

Yet fire is present; it seems to be all.

E il lupo

Quando scricchiola il ghiaccio
ed animali in ansia là sulla banchina
guardano i mari disfatti, la deriva di icebergs

e sussulti di squali trafittti dalla fiocina
s'agitano, si spengono e il salmone
avido di procreazione e moribondo
nuota a ritroso nei torrenti in piena

e il lupo
con spasimo di tutta la sua vita
di quella dei suoi padri e dei suoi cuccioli
con questa ressa nel cuore

prende la via dei monti e si ritrova
agile sulle vecchie zampe, pronto
al richiamo dei venti originari
che squillano l'amore il viaggio e la rapina,

vita non mia, dolore
che porto nella notte
e dal caos,
ti risenti improvvisa nel profondo,
ti torci nelle angustie, sotto il carico.

And the Wolf

When the ice creaks and animals in fear
on the banks look at the tumbling seas
and drifting icebergs

and harpooned sharks quiver and die
and, eager to give life, the wasting salmon
buck the torrential flow

and the wolf
with an anguish that's his
his ancestors' his cubs'
thus torn at heart

heads for the mountains and discovers
he's quick on his old legs,
ears cocked for the call of native winds
trumpeting love, the stalking and the kill

O life not mine,
pain I carry into the night from chaos,
suddenly you are yourself again
twisting in your chains under the load.

Vivere vivo come può chi serve

fedele poi che non ha scelta. Tutto,

anche la cupa eternità animale

che geme in noi può farsi santa. Basta

poco, quel poco taglia come spada.

To live alive like one who—no choice given—

faithfully serves: all, even the dark

immemorial beasts howling in us,

can be redeemed. It takes little, but

that little cuts like a sword.

Senior

Ai vecchi

tutto è troppo.

Una lacrima nella fenditura

della roccia può vincere

la sete quando è così scarsa. Fine

e vigilia della fine chiedono

poco, parlano basso.

Ma noi, nel pieno dell'età,

nella fornace dei tempi, noi? Pensaci.

Senior

To old men

everything is too much.

A tear in a fissure

of a rock can slake

their thirst when it is so small.

End's eve and the end ask for little,

speak softly.

But we in our prime,

we, in our burning time? Think of it.

GIORGIO CAPRONI

Giorgio Caproni was born in Leghorn in 1912 and spent much of his earlier years in his native city and then Genoa, where he published his first collection, *Come un'allegoria* ("Like an Allegory"), in 1936, followed by *Ballo a Fontanigorda, ibid.* (1938; "Dance in Fontanigorda, Ibid."). He fought in World War II on the western front, ultimately abandoning the Fascist Party to join the partisan resistance in Val Trebbia in Liguria. After the war, he moved to Rome, where he worked as a journalist, writer, and translator. Many of Caproni's earlier compilations are collected in *Il passaggio d'Enea* (1952; "Aeneas's Passage"), and his *Il seme del piangere* (1959; "The Root of Weeping") won the Premio Viareggio. Caproni died in Rome in 1990. As he was trained as a violinist, his poems are musical, using such stylistic elements as assonance, internal rhyme, and enjambment. Elusive voyages (like those of Aeneas and Ulysses) recur in his work, and cities (Leghorn, Genoa, Paris) are frequent characters. Poetic narrators are often estranged from their environs—much like the primate of "Il gibbone" ("The Gibbon")—and meaning and expression are based on what is unspeakable or absent rather than on what is tangible or apparent (e.g., in "Senza esclamativi" ["Without Exclamations"]).

Interludio

E intanto ho conosciuto l'Erebo
—l'inverno in una latteria.

Ho conosciuto la mia
Proserpina, che nella scialba
veste lavava all'alba
i nuvolosi bicchieri.

Ho conosciuto neri
tavoli—anime in fretta
posare la bicicletta
allo stipite e entrare
a perdersi fra i vapori.

E ho conosciuto rossori
indicibili—mani
di gelo sulla segatura
rancida, e senza figura
nel fumo la ragazza
che aspetta con la sua tazza
vuota la mia paura.

Interlude

Meanwhile, I have known Erebus—
wintertime in a milk bar.
My Proserpine I've known
washing, in a drab dress,
filmy glasses at dawn.

I have known sooty tables—
and harried robot souls
leaning their bikes on the door jamb,
walking in, vanishing in smoke.

And I have known
raw sores that make you scream—
frozen hands spreading stale
sawdust, and in the steam,
shapeless, a girl
with an empty cup, waiting
on my distress.

Il gibbone

a Rina

No, non è questo il mio
paese. Qua
—fra tanta gente che viene,
tanta gente che va—
io sono lontano e solo
(straniero) come
l'angelo in chiesa dove
non c'è Dio. Come,
allo zoo, il gibbone.

Nell'ossa ho un'altra città
che mi strugge. È là.
L'ho perduta. Città
grigia di giorno e, a notte,
tutta una scintillazione
di lumi—un lume
per ogni vivo, come,
qui al cimitero, un lume
per ogni morto. Città
cui nulla, nemmeno la morte
—mai,— mi ricondurrà.

The Gibbon

to Rina

No, this is not my country.
Here—among so
many people who come and go—
I'm far away and lonely
(a stranger) like the angel
in a church where there is
no God. Like, at the zoo,
the gibbon. In my bones

another city lies
that consumes me. Over there.
I have lost it. A city
gray by day and by night
a conflagration of lights—
a light for each living creature
as in a graveyard
there is one for each dead.

My city, to which nothing
ever, not even death,
will bring me back.

L'ora ormai della nottola

a Goffredo Petrassi

L'ora—ormai—della nottola.

Un'ora brusca.

L'ora
quando con i suoi fili
di silenzio, l'erba
della convalle strema
l'ultimo verde.

Un'ora
ad arma bianca.

L'ora
di taglio tra mano e volto, dove
anche l'acqua perde
il rumore, e appena
ne increspa la superficie
una voce che chiama.

Un'ora falcidiatrice.

Un acciaio.

Una lama.

Now the Time of the Bat

to Goffredo Petrassi

Now the time of the bat.

Abrupt.

The time
when with threadlets of silence
the valley's grass
exhausts its furthest green.

A time of hand-to-hand combat,

cutting between
hand and face, when
water loses its noise
and a calling voice barely
moves its surface.

A time

of mowing. Blades of

steel.

CRISTINA CAMPO

Cristina Campo, pseudonym for Vittoria Guerrini, was born in Bologna in 1923. From an early age she suffered from a heart defect, which caused her to be home-schooled and finally led to her death in Rome in 1977. She spent her early years in Bologna and Florence, then moved to Rome in 1955 to follow her father, who was the director of the Conservatory of Santa Cecilia. Campo was private about her writing, publishing only one volume of poetry while she was alive, *Passo d'addio* (1956; "The Farewell Passage"). Much of her writing was published posthumously in *La tigre assenza* (1991; "The Tiger Absence"), containing both poetry and translations; her prose is gathered in *Gli imperdonabili* (1987; "The Unforgivable Ones"). She was an avid translator, translating William Carlos Williams, John Donne, and Emily Dickinson, among many others. Her poetry has a liturgical function: it can both redeem and condemn, as in "Ora rivoglio bianche tutte le mie lettere" ("Now I want all my letters back, erased"). Religious mysticism is central to her work, and the poetic narrator often suffers physical and mental anguish in her attempt to render the beauty of the world (as in "Canone IV" ["Canon IV"]).

Ora rivoglio bianche...

Ora rivoglio bianche tutte le mie lettere,

inaudito il mio nome, la mia grazia richiusa;

ch'io mi distenda sul quadrante dei giorni,

riconduca la vita a mezzanotte.

E la mia valle rosata dagli uliveti

e la città intricata dei miei amori

siano richiuse come breve palmo,

il mio palmo segnato da tutte le mie morti.

O Medio Oriente disteso dalla sua voce,

voglio destarmi sulla via di Damasco—

né mai lo sguardo aver levato a un cielo

altro dal suo, da tanta gioia in croce.

Now I want all my letters back, . . .

Now I want all my letters back, erased,

my name unheard, my innocence walled in;

let me spread out over the face of time,

bring life back to midnight.

As to my valley immersed in olive groves,

my city of tangled loves—

let them be closed like my small palm,

my palm criss-crossed by death.

O Middle East created by His voice,

I want to awake on the road to Damascus—

and never ever redirect my eyes

to a sky not His, a bliss not of the cross.

devota come ramo...

devota come ramo
curvato da molte nevi
allegra come falò
per colline d'oblio,

su acutissime lame
in bianca maglia d'ortiche,
ti insegnerò, mia anima,
questo passo d'addio...

as devout as a branch . . .

as devout as a branch
bent down by many snows
wild as a bonfire
through ranges of oblivion

on razor blades, in a
horsehair shirt
I will teach you, my soul,
this farewell step . . .

Roberto Sanesi

Roberto Sanesi was born in 1930 in Milan and died there in 2001. His first collection of poetry, *Il feroce equilibrio* ("The Savage Equilibrium"), was published in 1957. Three years later he received the Byron Award and was subsequently invited to Harvard as poet in residence. A fervent writer, Sanesi worked as an essayist, journalist, art critic, novelist, and translator (among the authors he translated were Shakespeare, Dylan Thomas, and T. S. Eliot) and published more than twenty collections of poetry. He was also a painter, worked as a consultant for the Tate Gallery in London, and was involved with the opera (as a director, librettist, and curator). Other collections of his verse are *La cosa scritta* (1977; "The Written Thing"), *Recitazione obbligata* (1981; "Obligatory Recitation"), and *Mercurio* (1994; "Mercury"). Sanesi followed the visual writing movement of the 1960s, and his later poetry combined the written word and the image. Much of his work is metaphysical and abstract, and elements such as time, play, myth, and death frequently recur.

Anniversario

Melo di roseo vento il tempo suona,

accende fuochi e tentazioni il tempo,

e dice (non racconta), dice, come se in mezzo agli alberi,

alle foglie, non solo il vento fosse, il vento,

il tempo, con il suo capo ruvido di ruggine

a battere nei nodi e nelle mani il freddo, a chiudere

le porte gemendo ai mutamenti, sbadigliando,

e due di meno dico, e non vi sono colli

da risalire con lo svelto passo, o le chiarezze

delle stelle acerbe, o un vivo

vertice d'ignoranza sul mio viso ora

che in rigoroso parlamento vanno

emergendo dal buio rarefatte

le nebulose all'albe del gennaio. E due di meno

dico, due che graffiano a stento gli episodi

del poiché siamo e ciò che siamo e cosa

saremmo se non fossimo, e ricadono

in uno specchio fossile di giorni

dove l'età stratifica banale in rughe che non mutano

ogni volta nulla se non un correre di sguardi a rovescio

nel vento, e zampe di coniglio

portafortuna e capricorni inutili. Lo vedo. E due di meno

dico, e non so cosa

sia da cui trarre i due che già mi pesano.

Uccideremmo il mondo a questo modo.

Anniversary

Apple tree of rosy wind, time makes music, time
      rouses temptations, fires,
and says (tells not), says, as if among the trees,
the leaves, not only the wind were, the wind,
      time, with its head hoary with rust
hammering cold into knots and hands, closing doors groaning
at changes, yawning, and two less, I say,
      and no more hills
to climb again with quick steps, or sparkles of
      new stars, no throbbing
climax of ignorance on my face now
      that the austere conclave
of rarefied nebulae is emerging from the dark
      in the January dawns.
Two less, I say, two who barely scratch at facts
      of why we are and what we are and what
we'd be if we were not and fall back into
      a fossil mirror of days where age
trivially stratifies into wrinkles that don't change
each time anything but a run of backward glances
      in the wind, and rabbits' charmed paws
and useless capricorns. I see. And two less, I say
      and do not know from what
to subtract the two weighing me down
      already. We would kill the world this way.

Occhi di pane azzimo...

Occhi di pane azzimo ha la luna sopra
    i tetti viola, e al tuo balcone
una serenità inquietante ecco trasale simile a me ferita.

Come potei credermi allora illeso quando fra le tue
    palpebre fiorì
una luce che parve ripropormi tutte le età dell'uomo? Era
    una notte
tepida e dall'oriente un quieto vento frugava
    nella tua voce un sospiro, andava
trasvolando qua e là framezzo al Carro. Ora ti prego non mi
    dire quanto

mi tratterrai con questa muta fede, con questa luce d'ambra
    che mi getti
da lontananze o da crudeli insonnie di vita in cui il tuo
    viso si confonde.

Nell'alto azzurro carcere dell'aria, stretti là dove i
    passeri si lagnano
di troppa libertà, forse per noi qualcuno con le sue dita
    fragili ravvia

—dove placare, ancora vivi, l'anima—un prato
    d'impossibile silenzio.

The Moon Has Eyes of Matzo

On purple roofs, the moon has eyes of matzo,
      and on your balcony—
right there—a disquieting peace winces, wounded like me.

How could I then think myself unharmed when
      between your eyelids bloomed
a light that seemed to repropose to me
      all the ages of man? It was a warm

night and a gentle breeze from the East ruffled
      a whisper from your voice,
fluttering left and right across the Dipper. I beg you
      now do not tell me

how long you'll keep me with this speechless faith,
      this amber light you throw me from a distance,
away from these
      cruel nightmares of life where your face blurs.

In the high, blue prison of air, confined where
      sparrows complain
of too much freedom, perhaps for us someone
      with frail fingers is cutting

—grounds where, in the flesh, we would content our soul—
      a meadow of impossible silence.

ANDREA ZANZOTTO

Andrea Zanzotto was born in Pieve di Soligo, in the Veneto, in 1921, where he still lives. He began teaching when he was sixteen and graduated with a degree in literature from Padua in 1942. In his work—Zanzotto fought against Fascism as a member of the partisan resistance—he explores and contests Fascism as a regime and a mentality. The landscapes of his highly lyrical earlier collections, such as *Dietro il paesaggio* (1951; "Behind the Landscape"), represent a country devastated by war. Many poems are set in his native Veneto. Zanzotto is often referred to as an ontological poet, concerned with the nature of reality, and he is profoundly interested in how the individual, in contemporary society, is controlled by consumer media. In the ironic prologue to his poem "Sì, ancora la neve" ("Yes, the Snow Again," in *La Beltà* [1968; "Beauty"]) the child abandons his interest in ontology and wonder to focus on the material products obtained at the local drugstore. Zanzotto frequently employs dialect in his verse, and later collections, such as *Il galateo in bosco* (1979; "A Code of Manners in the Forest"), are highly experimental. *Sovrimpressioni* (2001; "Superimpressions"), his most recent collection, speaks to such pressing issues as the Bosnian conflict and the linguistic and environmental destruction of the Veneto.

Tu sei: mi trascura...

Tu sei: mi trascura

e tutto brividi mi lascia la stagione;

fragole a boschi e pomi a perdizione

nelle miriadi delle piogge

La pura estate consumata

dai grandi venti

illuminata dall'amore

e tutta un'altra fioritura

che non significa e non pesa

e questo pomeriggio improvvisato

perché da te mi possa congedare

Con te verde ora

di caligini e raggi

mi salvi, io vedo ancora

tra accecanti ricchezze.

You are, it neglects . . .

You are, it neglects
and leaves me all shuddering the season;
strawberries by the woods apples to infinity
in nebulae of rains

pure summer
consumed by the great winds
lit up by love

and quite another flowering
without meaning or weight
and this impromptu afternoon for me
to say good-bye to you

with you green now
with mists and rays
I'm saved, I still can see
among blinding possessions.

Colloquio

«Ora il sereno è ritornato le campane suonano per il vespero ed io le ascolto con grande dolcezza. Gli ucelli cantano festosi nel cielo perché? Tra poco e primavera i prati meteranno il suo manto verde, ed io come un fiore appasito guardo tutte queste meraviglie.»

Scritto su un muro in campagna

Per il deluso autunno,
per gli scolorenti
boschi vado apparendo, per la calma
profusa, lungi dal lavoro
e dal sudato male.

Teneramente
sento la dalia e il crisantemo
fruttificanti ovunque sulle spalle
del muschio, sul palpito sommerso
d'acque deboli e dolci.

Improbabile esistere di ora
in ora allinea me e le siepi
all'ultimo tremore
della diletta luna,
vocali foglie emana
l'intimo lume della valle. E tu
in un marzo perpetuo le campane

Conversation

"Now good weather is back bells ring the vespers and i listen to them
with great sweetness. Birds are singing happy in the sky, who knows
what for. In a short while it will be spring and meadows will put on a
green cape, and like a wilted flower i look at all these wonders."
(*written on a country wall*)

Through frustrated fall,
through fading woods,
through peace poured forth I walk,
away from work
and sweated evil.
Tenderly I feel
the dahlia and the chrysanthemum
everywhere bearing fruit upon the shoulders
of moss, on the submerged pulsating
of narrow and sweet waters.
Improbable existence
steadily summons me and the hedges
to the last trembling
of the beloved moon,
the valley's inner glow
emanates singing leaves.
And you in perpetual March the bells

dei Vesperi, la meraviglia

delle gemme e dei selvosi uccelli

e del languore, nel ripido muro

nella strofe scalfita ansimando m'accenni;

nel muro aperto da piogge e da vermi

il fortunato marzo

mi spieghi tu con umili

lontanissimi errori, a me nel vivo

d'ottobre altrimenti annientato

ad altri affanni attento.

Sola sarai, calce sfinita e segno,

sola sarai fin che duri il letargo

o s'ecciti la vita.

Io come un fiore appassito

guardo tutte queste meraviglie

E marzo quasi verde quasi

meriggio acceso di domenica

marzo senza misteri

inebetì nel muro.

of Vespers and the miracle of buds,
of sylvan birds and torpor, on the steep
wall in the lines
nicked out of breath you hint to me;
in the wall cracked by rains and worms
charmed March
you explain with humble
remote mistakes, in the heart of October
to me otherwise destroyed
on other pains intent.
You will be alone, exhausted lime and sign,
alone you'll be until lethargy lasts
or life is sparked.

like a wilted flower I
look at all these wonders

And almost green almost
noon with a touch of Sunday
March without mysteries

stood dazzled on a wall.

Retorica su: Lo sbandamento, il principio 'Resistenza'

III

Orientarsi poco, in tutto. Essere in disordine

essere per forza morti e spesso

dichiaratamente

retorici e sciocchi o miseramente

vicini vicini all'orientamento.

Oh retorico amore

opera-fascino.

Non saltare e saltare al di là di questo cerchio

non promuoversi e promuoversi oltre.

Ardeva il fascino e la realtà

conversando convergendo

horeb ardevi tutto d'arbusti

tutto arbusto horeb il mondo ardeva.

E aveva una sola parola

(non è vero, no,

questa espressione è la punta di diamante

del retorizzamento, lo scolice della

sacramentale contraddizione,

ma vedi come ne sono...)

male ascoltata

bene ascoltata

una sola parola che diceva

e diceva il dire

e diceva il che. E. Congiungere. Con.

Rhetoric On: Straying, the "Resistance"

III

To scarcely get one's bearings in everything.

To be messed up and dead on purpose

and often admittedly rhetorical

and silly or pitifully

so close to the right path.

Oh rhetorical love

awe-work.

Not to keep jumping beyond the circle

not to push one's case further and further.

Awe was burning and talking

tightening reality

Horeb you were one blaze of bushes

all bush Horeb the world was burning.

And it had just one word

(not true, no, this expression

is the diamond tip of rhetorizing,

the tapeworm's head of the holy contradiction,

but see that I am full of it? . . .)

heard

and not heard

one single word that kept on

speaking the spoken

and spoke the what. And. To link. With.

Torna, dove sei?

Torna: nel seno della cremazione

dai fieni cremati

torna io-noi, Hölderlin,

dipana il semplice sempre più semplice,

corri corri arrivano;

battaglione lepre, brigata coniglio,

all'assalto: è il tempo

dell'opus maxime oratorium.

Una riga tremante Hölderlin fammi scrivere.

Sì? Nel fascino tutto conversa converge?

IV

E ho mangiato anche quel giorno

—dopo il sangue—

e mangio tutti i giorni

—dopo l'insegnamento—

una zuppa gustosa, fagioli.

Posso farlo e devo.

Tutti possono e devono.

Bello. Fagiolo. Fiore.

Come back, where are you?

Come back: to the womb of cremation

from cremated hays come back

I-we, Hölderlin,

unravel the simple to greater simplicity,

run run they're here;

hare battalion, rabbit brigade,

on the attack: it is the time

of opus maxime oratorium.

One trembling line Hölderlin make me write.

Yes? Do in awe all things tighten and talk?

IV

And I ate even after that day

—after the blood—

and I eat every day

—after teaching—

a tasty soup, with beans.

I eat and must.

Everyone can and must.

Lovely. Bean. Flower.

Realistic Experimentation

Sibilla Aleramo

The poet, novelist, and critic Sibilla Aleramo (pseudonym for Rina Faccio) was born in Alessandria, in Piedmont, in 1876. She lived in Milan until 1881, when her family moved to the Marches, where her father managed a factory and where she worked as a bookkeeper. At fifteen she was raped by a factory employee, whom she later married. This experience scarred her, and she began to write for such feminist publications as *L'Italia femminile* ("Woman's Italy"), which she briefly directed. During her marriage she suffered from severe depression and attempted suicide. She left her husband and son in 1902 to move to Rome, where she was actively engaged with the women's and the workers' movements. She wrote the highly successful autobiographical novel *Una donna* (1906; "A Woman"), a sharp criticism of patriarchal institutions. Aleramo had a series of illustrious, at times stormy, relationships with such intellectuals as Giovanni Cena and Dino Campana. Her poetry is collected in *Selva d'amore* (1947; "Woods of Love"), and she continued to write novels until her death in Rome in 1960. Themes of death, love, old age, fear, and anguish recur in her work. She believed that life and art are inseparable. Her poems, written in an improvised, anguished language, externalize inner torments and conflicts.

Son tanto brava...

Son tanto brava lungo il giorno.

Comprendo, accetto, non piango.

Quasi imparo ad aver orgoglio quasi fossi un uomo.

Ma, al primo brivido di viola in cielo

ogni diurno sostegno dispare.

Tu mi sospiri lontano: «Sera, sera dolce e mia!»

Sembrami d'aver fra le dita

la stanchezza di tutta la terra.

Non son più che sguardo, sguardo sperduto, e vene.

I am so good . . .

I am so good all day long.

I understand, accept, do not cry—

almost emanate pride

as if I were a man.

But at first shock of violet in the sky

all the day's strength vanishes.

Far off you whisper to me:

"Evening, so sweet and mine!"

Not so. In my hands

I hold the weariness of the world.

I'm only a lost person glanced at, and nerves.

Amalia Guglielminetti

Amalia Guglielminetti was born in Turin in 1881 into a well-off family and received a religious education. The death of her father early in her life deeply affected her, and she dedicated *Voci di giovinezza* ("Voices of Youth"), her first volume of poetry, to him in 1903. In 1907 she published *Le vergini folli* ("The Mad Virgins"), which caught the attention of the poet Guido Gozzano, and their correspondence led to an intense love affair, which was documented by her posthumous *Lettere d'amore* (1951; "Love Letters"). Guglielminetti directed a literary journal (*Seduzioni* ["Seductions"]) and wrote children's stories and several novels. Two of the novels, *Quando avevo un amante* ("When I Had a Lover") and *La rivincita del maschio* ("The Male's Revenge"), both published in 1923, were declared obscene by the League of Public Morality. Guglielminetti suffered from bouts of depression throughout her life. She died in 1941 from injuries sustained during an air raid in Turin. Her poetry and prose often defy traditional perspectives on gender. Sensual poems such as "La mia voce" ("My Voice") and "Bellezza della vita" ("Life's Beauty") are written in a feminine language that critiques the status quo.

La mia voce

La mia voce non ha rombo di mare

o d'echi alti tra fughe di colonne:

ma il susurro che par fruscío di gonne

con cui si narran femminili gare.

Io non volli cantar, volli parlare,

e dir cose di me, di tante donne

cui molti desideri urgon l'insonne

cuore e lascian con labbra un poco amare.

E amara è pur la mia voce talvolta,

quasi vi tremi un riso d'ironia,

più pungente a chi parla che a chi ascolta.

Come quando a un'amica si confida

qualche segreto di malinconia

e si ha paura ch'ella ne sorrida.

My Voice

My voice is not the roar of the sea
or a deep echo through flights of columns:
rather it murmurs—a rustle of skirts
whispering female grudges.

I did not want to sing, I wanted to speak,
to speak about myself and all those women
whose countless wishes arouse their sleepless hearts
and leave them with mildly bitter lips.

And bitter too is my voice at times,
almost quivering with a smile of irony,
more biting to the speaker than the listener.

As when we entrust to a friend
some melancholy secret,
afraid that she will smile at it.

CARLO BETOCCHI

Carlo Betocchi was born in Turin in 1899 into a Catholic family. His Catholic faith held a central place in his life and work. When he was seven, he moved to Florence with his parents. In 1917 he fought in World War I, and in 1918 he volunteered to serve in Libya. After returning from Africa, he worked as a land surveyor, in 1929 cofounded the Florentine Catholic Hermetic review *Frontespizio* ("Frontispiece"), and in 1932 published his first collection of poetry, *Realtà vince il sogno* ("Reality Defeats Dream"). Betocchi spent most of his life in Florence, where he continued writing poetry—other collections are *L'estate di San Martino* (1961; "Indian Summer") and *Un passo, un altro passo* (1967; "Step by Step")—until his death in Bordighera in 1986. He won several literary prizes, including the Premio Viareggio (1955) and the Montale-Guggenheim Prize (1984). His earlier poetry is frequently classified as hermetic, although, as is evident in the title of his first collection, reality (always based in Catholic devotion) is preferred to fantasy. Pastoral settings reappear in his work, and the poetic narrator frequently contemplates his surroundings and realizes his place in the divine order.

E ne dondola il ramo

Di che improvvise croci

empiamo l'aria con l'ali
degli opposti pensieri: con che disegni
fallaci, se pur nati sinceri,
ti disegnamo, divina pace,

tentandoti, o difficile equilibrio...
E ne dondola il ramo, mentre
tra verdi foglie ebbri sentieri
si spalancano. O eternità,

che come i trabocchetti
della vita ci attiri! o passi,
lenti come l'autunno sui campi,
o limo del paradiso che c'impanii!

And the Branch Swings with It

With what amazing crosses
do we cut air with wings
of our contrasting thoughts; with what imperfect
drawings though born sincere

do we sketch you, God's peace,
trying to reach a balance.
And the branch swings with it
while through green leaves dizzying paths appear.

O eternity that like
life's pitfalls calls us.
Steps slow as autumn in the fields; O lime
of paradise that coaxes us.

A cuci e scuci,...

A cuci e scuci, dicono i muratori
quel metter le mani a un muro che si sgretola,
antico, e rappezzarlo a frammenti:
e dentro i vecchi pertugi dell'anima
così mi canticchia una lunga pazienza.

Patch it here . . .

Patch it here and patch it there
masons call setting their hands
to a collapsing wall and fixing it
by piecemeal: so
in the old crannies of my soul
enduring patience sings.

Un passo, un altro passo,...

Un passo, un altro passo,

ivi del cielo il masso

azzurro, la vivente natura,

e l'inferma pietà

che se stessa conosce negli errori,

e la lieve follia, ivi la morte,

il rumore e il silenzio,

e il mio esistere anonimo;

e come dalla pietra sale il canto

di un colore che è muto,

un passo, un altro passo,

e inciampicando nel divino esistere

io giungo a riconoscermi nel sasso

che sospira all'eterno, in alto, in basso.

Step by step, . . .

Step by step,
there lies the sky's blue core,
nature, and meek compassion
that knows itself in errors;
there lies light folly,
noise, death, and silence—
my secluded existence.

As song rises from stone,
its tonality speechless,
step by step—
stumbling into divinity
I come to recognize myself
in the stone that strains upward,
downward, to its eternity.

Franco Fortini

Franco Fortini was born Franco Lattes in 1917 in Florence, where he received two degrees, in law and art history. In 1940, to avoid persecution under Mussolini's racial laws, Fortini adopted his mother's last name. She was a Catholic. The same year, he was forced into the army as a second lieutenant, where he served for two years before deserting and fleeing to Switzerland. He returned to Italy to join the partisan resistance. After the war, he moved to Milan (where he published his first poetry collection, *Foglio di via e altri versi* (1946; "'Expulsion Order' and Other Poems") and became involved in politics. He edited political journals such as *Avanti!* ("Go Ahead!") and *Comunità* ("Community") and was active in the Socialist Party until 1957, when he left, protesting that the party was divided, to begin advocating a new left in Italy. Fortini worked as a translator, journalist, critic, and editor and taught history at the University of Siena for several years. In 1985 he won the prestigious Montale-Guggenheim Prize. He died in Milan in 1994. Often thought of as an ideological poet, he is politically and socially engaged. In *Poesia ed errore* (1959; "Poems and Errors") he recalls the experience of war. Elsewhere, as in *Una volta per sempre* (1973; "Once and for All"), the poet considers communism and various social injustices.

Prologo ai vicini

Che cosa importa se non mi vogliono bene
se vanno lontani da me.
L'amicizia è d'un altro tempo.

Che cosa importa se anch'io non li amo
se non ho prudenza e pazienza.
Anche il tempo è d'un altro tempo.

Ma dietro queste nuvole di nulla e neve salgono
tranquilli soli concordi cuori.
Che cosa importa se non li vedo ancora.

Da questo luogo io sorridendo resisto.
Dunque era vero che sarebbe stata
ogni cosa come previsto inflessibile

che invisibile agli occhi inaccessibile al cuore
sarebbe stato il reale e il possibile
e per nuda fede avrei dovuto confessarlo.

Ergo qui sto e di qui amaramente parlo.
Che cosa importa se non mi vogliono bene
che cosa importa se anch'io non li amo.

Qualche rosa della mente m'inghirlanda la neve.

Prologue to the Neighbors

What does it matter if they do not love me
and move away from me.
Friendship belongs to another time.

What does it matter if I do not love them
and have neither wisdom nor patience.
Even time belongs to another time.

But behind these clouds and drifts of snow
peaceful hearts alone in concord glow.
What does it matter if I don't see them yet.

From this plot smiling I endure.
So it was true. Everything was to be
hard as predicted:

the real and the possible invisible
to the eye and for the heart unreachable—
true that I would accept this in blind faith.

So I stand here and so my bitter speech.
What does it matter if they do not love me.
What does it matter if I do not love them.

The roses in my mind make snow a bower.

Giardino d'estate, Pechino

Ora su questo paese è venuto l'autunno,

calma la ruota ora la parte d'ombra,

e chi fruga nei campi vede tumuli e fumi

che tramutano alla pioggia.

Qui, per mano, tepore

che si cede e si serba,

a frotte uomini turchini

scendono scogli e grotte,

sfiorano gru di bronzo, fenici distrutte.

Ospiti miti della terra, guardano

i salici, le nebbie, i melograni

nei parchi della lunga festa del primo ottobre.

Presto sarò tornato

dove non è mai stato questo giorno

e là, chiuse le imposte,

anche il vostro tepore sarà il mio,

ogni sera all'inverno

come voi sarò un uomo di pazienza.

Altro fra noi? Scendete

a coppie, a gruppi, geni benevoli, corpi

del passato o dell'avvenire...

Ogni cosa fu detta, il pesce e il monte,

la campana di guerra, il vino e il pianto,

Summer Garden, Beijing

Now fall has come over this country,

wheels steady now as the contours of shade;

roaming the fields, one sees

clouds of smoke and mounds

changing under the rain. Here, hand in hand,

warmth is both kept and given,

clusters of bright blue men

climb down rocks into grottoes,

brush on bronze cranes, phoenixes that lie wrecked.

Mild guests of the earth, they look at willows,

fogs and pomegranates in the parks

of the long holiday of October First.

Soon I'll be back

where this day never was

and there, my shutters closed,

your warmth too will be mine,

every evening in winter

I'll be like you a man of perseverance.

Nothing more between us? Come down in pairs

or groups, dear home divinities,

bodies belonging to the past, the future . . .

We said it all, the fish and the mountain,

the war gong, tears, the wine,

e questo lago dove barche vanno

tanto sottili che un giunco le cela.

Basta un attimo solo a non esistere—

ma nulla in me, in nessuno, s'interrompe

finché, remoti, siete anche per me.

O si ripete o si muta o si salva.

E dunque tutto ancora

si può dire una volta

nelle sere che a noi guardano ancora,

miei padri, figli, mia sola famiglia.

and this lake where boats glide—

so slender that a rush can hide them.

It only takes an instant to stop living,

but nothing breaks in me or anyone

so long as, even from afar, you exist for me.

Else it's renewed, or modified, or saved.

And so everything

can be said once again

in the evenings that are still left for us,

O fathers, children, my only family.

Sonetto

Debole spirito alito tenace
ch'abiti dove più buia è la mente
dove ogni grido scende nella pace
e i giorni chiusi, l'erbe e i visi spenti

tu non lasciarmi ora che intendo quanti
pochi anni ancora ormai andrò nel giorno.
Parte di me già copre l'ombra; e sperde
le cose, se le mani tendo, in polvere.

Tu appena un fiato sei della mia polvere.
Come alle fronde ferme nelle notti
d'afa dall'aria sottili parole

parole ancora dal fondo dei sonni
so che anzi l'alba mi rechi. Ma il giorno
non le ritrova, e non ti riconosco.

Sonnet

Firefly spirit and undying breath
who lives where the intellect is darkest
where every cry descends into peace
with ended days, grasses and pallid faces

do not leave me now that I understand
how few more years I will walk in the day.
Shade already covers a good part of me; it routs
things into dust, if I stretch my hands out.

Today you are only that breath of my dust.
As to still fronds in the hot, sultry nights
from the air an unexpected murmur sighs

words yet from the spring well of my dreams
I know you bring me before dawn. But day
can't find them, and you're not what you have been.

PIER PAOLO PASOLINI

Pier Paolo Pasolini, one of the most controversial intellectual figures of the twentieth century, was born in Bologna in 1922. He spent his early years in various cities (his father was in the military) and studied literature at the University of Bologna before moving to Friuli, his mother's homeland, in 1943. He began writing poetry, in dialect and otherwise, at an early age. His brother, a member of the partisan resistance, was killed by Yugoslav Communists in 1945. In 1949, Pasolini moved to Rome, where he worked as a teacher in the Roman *borgate* ("slums"). His public life as a Marxist, homosexual, and Catholic made him a contentious figure. His personal life was constantly put on trial, as his public homosexuality threatened conservative ideologies of gender identification. As a poet, novelist, dramatist, screenwriter, director, journalist, and critic, he was involved in every aspect of cultural life. In 1975, he was murdered by a young man whom he picked up in Rome; the motive remained unknown. Pasolini is a civil poet, engaging political, social, and ethical tensions. Earlier collections such as *Le ceneri di Gramsci* (1957; "Gramsci's Ashes"), set in the squalor of the *borgate*, present his revitalizing *ragazzi di vita* ("vivacious and resilient boys"). His final collection, *Trasumanar e organizzar* (1971; "Transhumanize and Organize"), is ideologically grounded.

Al sole

No, non a noi: tu manchi

a loro, che pure vivono a livelli

d'esistenza di sole, in pienezza,

e tra baracche e sterri,

sentono in questa disorientata brezza

con altro cuore, il tuo non esserci.

Si son rimessi cappottini e scialle

sulle umiliate spalle,

e aspettano appoggiati

battendo i piedi sui selciati sconnessi,

il vecchio auto dei loro caseggiati,

come muti, impotenti carcerati.

Urlerei, colpito da non so che dolore.

Solo la tristezza di un giorno nemico

mi unisce a questa grande vita morta.

Nel tuo buio, sole,

si compie ancora una volta l'ingiustizia:

per essi, che son senza

vestiti a casa, per me,

che soffro mistica degradazione.

Non so, ora, quale sia

il problema. Non so se conti averne

in questa terra abbandonata

To the Sun

We don't miss you, they do

who still bloom in the sun

and between shacks and bulldozed fields

in this misguided breeze

feel your absence with a different spirit.

On bowed shoulders they wear

worn-out coats, faded scarves.

Huddled they wait, like helpless, mute inmates,

for the old neighborhood bus

tapping their feet on cracked sidewalks.

I could scream, struck by pain.

Only the grayness of a day like this

links me to this great, dead life.

In your shadow, sun,

injustice once more is enacted:

to those who are naked in their homes,

to me in my intellectual degradation.

Right now I don't know where the problem is.

I don't know if it's worth having one

in this land abandoned to meaningless,

alle sue insignificanti, eterne

vicende di sole e di foschia.

Non so se posso tornare alla superata

angoscia, e per quale nuova strada,

o imparare i modi

della contemplazione,

all'ombra di una nuova lotta, e ai sordidi

inviti del nuovo capitale, già padrone

un'altra volta, e disposto al perdono...

Ho saputo, eccome ho saputo!,

da ragazzo, quello che dovevo essere

e che dovevo fare: tutto. Allora

il mio mondo di ossesso

era il mondo del capitale: ero perduto

in esso come nel suo frutto un sapore,

come un tepore nella tua luce, sole.

Obbediente, sincero, atterrito,

non dovevo essere buono, ma santo,

non uomo, ma gigante,

non elegante, ma puro, squisito.

Dovevo cercare un linguaggio,

e esprimere quel mio intimo lume infinito,

che fosse estremo: ingenuo appannaggio

dell'agio borghese, dell'antiborghese coraggio.

Ho saputo, eccome ho saputo!,

ventenne, capire quale era il sentimento

eternal successions of mist and sun.

I don't know whether I can go back

to dismissed anguish, and by which path;

whether to sharpen my mind against a new hatred

or to learn how to meditate

on the sidelines of a new struggle,

the enticements of the new state,

once more master and inclined to forgiveness . . .

I knew, and how, as a boy,

what I should do and be: everything.

Then, obsessed by the world of money,

I was lost in it like a flavor in its fruit,

like a warmth in your light, sun.

Obedient, sincere, terrified,

I was not to be good, but holy;

not a man, but a giant;

not elegant, but exquisite, pure.

I needed a language of extremes

to give shape to my inward endless glow—

naive privilege of bourgeois

comfort, antibourgeois courage.

I knew, and how, at twenty,

which feeling was the strongest

più forte in quel luminoso caos di ogni sentimento:

la libertà. Era rimasto muto

per anni, e ora era un doloroso canto,

improvviso, assoluto. E quanto

è mutato il senso della nostra esistenza!

Ricordo, di quei tempi, solo la tua luce,

alta, sopra le perdute

radure del Friuli, sopra una gente senza

speranza: risplendevi puro,

sempre, eri l'acerba luce della Resistenza.

In un tempo che mai al mondo fu più scuro

eri l'acerba luce del futuro.

Ho saputo, eccome ho saputo!,

che dopo ogni impegno c'è di nuovo

il vuoto, e occorre altro impegno:

che ogni stato promuove

altro stato, e ciò che si è conosciuto

attraverso il dolore e lo sdegno

si rifà sconosciuto, nel dolore e lo sdegno.

Mentre ognuno con fede ricattatoria

era pieno della luce della sua scelta,

io continuavo per la strada incerta

della conoscenza, nell'ombra-luce della storia.

Intransigenza e dolore

erano solo garanzia di qualche vittoria,

e proprio dentro la tua luce di sole

fatto simbolo, serbavo il tuo furore.

in that luminous chaos of all feelings:

freedom. It had remained voiceless

for years and now was a dejected song,

absolute, sudden. How

the meaning of our life changed!

Of those days I remember only the light

high above the endless plains

of Friuli, above a hopeless people:

you shone clear, steady,

you were the unformed light of the Resistance.

At a time that never was darker

you were the unformed light of the future.

I knew, and how, that after

each commitment there's nothingness again,

so we must find another;

that each state brings on a new one

and what we learn through pain and indignation

becomes unknown in pain and indignation.

While everyone justified all

in the halo of his chosen faith,

I was trudging along the blurred road of history.

Intransigence and agony

were the only proof of victory

and in your very fire, made

a symbol, sun, I kept mine.

E non so più, ora, quale sia

il problema. L'angoscia non è più

segno di vittoria: il mondo vola

verso sue nuove gioventù,

ogni strada è finita, anche la mia.

Come ogni vecchio, io lo nego: sola

consolazione per chi, se trema, muore.

Negando il mondo, io nego le sue ere,

o provo per esse furia indiscriminata,

vedendo contaminata

ognuna d'esse da un'uguale miseria.

Tu splendi sopra un sogno,

buio sole: chi vuole non sapere,

vuole sognare...

Now I don't know what the problem is.

Anguish is no longer a sign

of victory, the world is rallying

around the young, every path is ended.

Even mine. Like any old man,

I deny it—the only comfort

for those who die when they exist in fear.

Denying the world, I deny its new eras,

or feel for them indiscriminate fury

stained as I see them all

by the same tawdriness.

Dark sun, you shine over a dream:

whoever doesn't want to know, eats dreams . . .

Le ceneri di Gramsci

1

Non è di maggio questa impura aria
che il buio giardino straniero
fa ancora più buio, o l'abbaglia

con cieche schiarite... questo cielo
di bave sopra gli attici giallini
che in semicerchi immensi fanno velo

alle curve del Tevere, ai turchini
monti del Lazio... Spande una mortale
pace, disamorata come i nostri destini,

tra le vecchie muraglie l'autunnale
maggio. In esso c'è il grigiore del mondo,
la fine del decennio in cui ci appare

tra le macerie finito il profondo
e ingenuo sforzo di rifare la vita;
il silenzio, fradicio e infecondo...

Tu giovane, in quel maggio in cui l'errore
era ancora vita, in quel maggio italiano
che alla vita aggiungeva almeno ardore,

Gramsci's Ashes

1

This impure air that the dark foreign garden

makes even darker, or stuns it

with dazzling light, is not

really May . . . this sky of filaments

over the yellow mansards

that in immense semicircles conceal

the Tiber's tortuousness, the purple

mountains of Latium . . . On the ancient walls

autumnal May pours out a mortal peace

as disaffected as our destinies.

In it there is the grayness of the world,

the decade's end in which we see

buried in ruins the absorbed

and naive effort to remake existence;

silence, sterile and sodden . . .

Young man, in that May where even mistakes

were life, in that Italian May

that at least added enthusiasm to life,

quanto meno sventato e impuramente sano

dei nostri padri—non padre, ma umile

fratello—già con la tua magra mano

delineavi l'ideale che illumina

(ma non per noi: tu, morto, e noi

morti ugualmente, con te, nell'umido

giardino) questo silenzio. Non puoi,

lo vedi?, che riposare in questo sito

estraneo, ancora confinato. Noia

patrizia ti è intorno. E, sbiadito,

solo ti giunge qualche colpo d'incudine

dalle officine del Testaccio, sopito

nel vespro: tra misere tettoie, nudi

mucchi di latta, ferrivecchi, dove

cantando vizioso un garzone già chiude

la sua giornata, mentre intorno spiove.

2

Tra i due mondi, la tregua, in cui non siamo.

Scelte, dedizioni... altro suono non hanno

ormai che questo del giardino gramo

e nobile, in cui caparbio l'inganno

che attutiva la vita resta nella morte.

Nei cerchi dei sarcofaghi non fanno

how less foolish and amorally healthy
than our fathers—not a father, but humble
brother—already with your bony hand

traced the ideal that illuminates
this silence (but not for us: you, dead,
and us equally dead, with you

in the damp garden). See? You cannot do
anything else but rest in this extraneous
place, still pinned down.

Patrician boredom is around you. Only
anvil blows, muffled, reach you
from the Testaccio workshops, sound asleep

at vespers in the midst of crumbling sheds,
bare mounds of tin, scrap iron,
where, singing, a dissolute shop boy

fast ends his day, as rain begins to fall.

  2
Between two worlds a truce, but not for us.
Choices, commitments . . . make no other sound
than this of the unhappy

and noble garden, in which dogged delusion
that tempered life persists in death.
In the ring of sarcophagi the lay

che mostrare la superstite sorte

di gente laica le laiche iscrizioni

su queste grige pietre, corte

e imponenti. Ancora di passioni

sfrenate senza scandalo son arse

le ossa dei miliardari di nazioni

più grandi; ronzano, quasi mai scomparse,

le ironie dei principi, dei pederasti,

i cui corpi sono nell'urne sparse

inceneriti e non ancora casti.

Qui il silenzio della morte è fede

di un civile silenzio di uomini rimasti

uomini, di un tedio che nel tedio

del Parco, discreto muta: e la città

che, indifferente, lo confina in mezzo

a tuguri e a chiese, empia nella pietà,

vi perde il suo splendore. La sua terra

grassa di ortiche e di legumi dà

questi magri cipressi, questa nera

umidità che chiazza i muri intorno

a smorti ghirigori di bosso, che la sera

inscriptions on the short, gray, and imposing
slabs only show the fate
of lay folk who survived.

The bones of billionaires
of greater nations are still burning
with unreined passions, and no scandal;

the ironies of princes, pedophiles,
whose bodies, not yet chaste,
are turned to ashes in the various urns,

still buzz, never completely obliterated.
Here the silence of death
is faith of a civil silence

of men who remained men, of an ennui
which, in the Park's ennui, discreetly changes:
and the city which indifferent bounds it

in the midst of hovels and churches, impious
in its piety, loses there its splendor.
Its soil, rich with legumes and nettles, bears

these slender cypress trees, this somber dampness
that stains the walls around
pale flourishes of boxwood, that the evening

rasserenando spegne in disadorni

sentori d'alga... quest'erbetta stenta

e inodora, dove violetta si sprofonda

l'atmosfera, con un brivido di menta,

o fieno marcio, e quieta vi prelude

con diurna malinconia, la spenta

trepidazione della notte. Rude

di clima, dolcissimo di storia, è

tra questi muri il suolo in cui trasuda

altro suolo; questo umido che

ricorda altro umido; e risuonano

—familiari da latitudini e

orizzonti dove inglesi selve coronano

laghi spersi nel cielo, tra praterie

verdi come fosforici biliardi o come

smeraldi: «And O ye Fountains...»—le pie

invocazioni...

3

Uno straccetto rosso, come quello

arrotolato al collo ai partigiani

e, presso l'urna, sul terreno cereo,

clearing up drowns in modest
effluvia of algae . . . this stunted, odorless
grass, where the purplish air slumps down,

with a whisper of mint,
or rotten hay, and the
spent trepidation of night quietly

preludes it with diurnal melancholy.
Among these walls the ground
in which more ground's distilled

wields a rough climate, perfumed with history;
this dampness which recalls
more dampness; and the pious invocations

familiarly resound from latitudes
and horizons where English woods crown lakes
lost in the sky, through prairies

green like phosphoric billiards
or emeralds: "And O ye fountains . . ."

3

A small red kerchief, like the one
knotted around the Partisans' necks
and, near the urn, on the waxen terrain,

diversamente rossi, due gerani.

Lì tu stai, bandito e con dura eleganza

non cattolica, elencato tra estranei

morti: Le Ceneri di Gramsci... Tra speranza

e vecchia sfiducia, ti accosto, capitato

per caso in questa magra serra, innanzi

alla tua tomba, al tuo spirito restato

quaggiù tra questi liberi. (O è qualcosa

di diverso, forse, di più estasiato

e anche di più umile, ebbra simbiosi

d'adolescente di sesso con morte...)

E, da questo paese in cui non ebbe posa

la tua tensione, sento quale torto

—qui nella quiete delle tombe—e insieme

quale ragione—nell'inquieta sorte

nostra—tu avessi stilando le supreme

pagine nei giorni del tuo assassinio.

Ecco qui ad attestare il seme

non ancora disperso dell'antico dominio,

questi morti attaccati a un possesso

che affonda nei secoli il suo abominio

two geraniums, of a different red.
There you lie, banished, with a stern
non-Catholic finesse, listed among

foreign dead: Gramsci's Ashes . . .
With hope and old delusion I draw near,
having stumbled upon this lean greenhouse,

before your tomb, your spirit that resided
down here with these free people.
(Or is it something else, perhaps—more witching

and also humbler, an adolescent's giddy
mixture of sex and death . . .)
And in this land, where your agitation

never relented, I feel how wrong you were
(here in the calmness of the graves), how right
(in that unruly fate of ours)

when you drew up momentous pages
in the days of your murder.
And here they are—to certify the seed

not yet dispersed of the ancient rule—
these dead stuck to a possession
that seeps through centuries its abomination

e la sua grandezza: e insieme, ossesso,

quel vibrare d'incudini, in sordina,

soffocato e accorante—dal dimesso

rione—ad attestarne la fine.

Ed ecco qui me stesso... povero, vestito

dei panni che i poveri adocchiano in vetrine

dal rozzo splendore, e che ha smarrito

la sporcizia delle più sperdute strade,

delle panche dei tram, da cui stranito

è il mio giorno: mentre sempre più rade

ho di queste vacanze, nel tormento

del mantenermi in vita; e se mi accade

di amare il mondo non è che per violento

e ingenuo amore sensuale

così come, confuso adolescente, un tempo

l'odiai, se in esso mi feriva il male

borghese di me borghese: e ora, scisso

—con te—il mondo, oggetto non appare

di rancore e quasi di mistico

disprezzo, la parte che ne ha il potere?

Eppure senza il tuo rigore, sussisto

and greatness: and together with it, maddening,

the vibrato of dulled anvils,

smothered, distressing,

from the poor quarter to seal its demise.

And here I am, myself . . . poor, clad in clothes

that the poor ogle in shopwindows

raw in their splendor: I, who have forgotten

the squalor of the most forsaken streets,

of trolley seats from which

my day is alienated: I enjoy

fewer and fewer holidays like this,

in the torment of just staying alive;

and if I happen to love the world, I do it

through a naive, violent, sensual love

just as, one day, a confused adolescent,

I hated it when the bourgeois evil of me,

a bourgeois, wounded me; and now that the world,

because of you, is split, doesn't the part

that has it in its power seem an object

of rancor and almost esoteric contempt?

And yet without your rigor, I go on

perchè non scelgo. Vivo nel non volere

del tramontato dopoguerra: amando

il mondo che odio—nella sua miseria

sprezzante e perso—per un oscuro scandalo

della coscienza...

4

Lo scandalo del contraddirmi, dell'essere

con te e contro te; con te nel cuore,

in luce, contro te nelle buie viscere;

del mio paterno stato traditore

—nel pensiero, in un'ombra di azione—

mi so ad esso attaccato nel calore

degli istinti, dell'estetica passione;

attratto da una vita proletaria

a te anteriore, è per me religione

la sua allegria, non la millenaria

sua lotta: la sua natura, non la sua

coscienza; è la forza originaria

dell'uomo, che nell'atto s'è perduta,

a darle l'ebbrezza della nostalgia,

una luce poetica: ed altro più

not choosing. I live in the inaction
of the waned postwar period:
loving the world I hate—scornful and lost

in its paltriness—all because my conscience
is mysteriously scandalized . . .

4

The scandal of denying myself, of being
with you and against you; with you in my heart,
when lucid, against you in the dark of my bowels;

a traitor of my paternal state
—in thought, in a shadow of action—
I feel one with it in the coziness

of instincts, of aesthetic passion;
drawn to a proletarian life
prior to you, to me its gaiety

is a creed, not its millennial struggle:
its nature, not its conscience;
it is man's primal strength,

that got lost in the act,
that leaves it with the rapture of nostalgia,
with a poetic light: and if I added

io non so dirne, che non sia

giusto ma non sincero, astratto

amore, non accorante simpatia...

Come i poveri povero, mi attacco

come loro a umilianti speranze,

come loro per vivere mi batto

ogni giorno. Ma nella desolante

mia condizione di diseredato,

io possiedo: ed è il più esaltante

dei possessi borghesi, lo stato

più assoluto. Ma come io possiedo la storia,

essa mi possiede; ne sono illuminato:

ma a che serve la luce?

5

Non dico l'individuo, il fenomeno

dell'ardore sensuale e sentimentale...

altri vizi esso ha, altro è il nome

e la fatalità del suo peccare...

Ma in esso impastati quali comuni,

prenatali vizi, e quale

anything more it would be
correct but insincere,
abstract love, not heartfelt empathy . . .

Poor like the poor, like them I clutch
at mortifying hopes;
like them, so as to live, I fight

every day. Yet in my desolate
disinherited status, I do own:
and it's the most exhilarating

of bourgeois possessions, the most absolute state.
But just as I own history,
it owns me; through it I am enlightened:

what difference does it make?

     5
I am not talking about the individual—
the phenomenon of sensual, mawkish ardor . . . —
he has more vices, the name and the fatality

of his sinning are different . . .
But mixed with him what common,
prenatal vices, what objective sin!

oggettivo peccato! Non sono immuni

gli interni e esterni atti, che lo fanno

incarnato alla vita, da nessuna

delle religioni che nella vita stanno,

ipoteca di morte, istituite

a ingannare la luce, a dar luce all'inganno.

Destinate a esser seppellite

le sue spoglie al Verano, è cattolica

la sua lotta con esse: gesuitiche

le manie con cui dispone il cuore;

e ancor più dentro: ha bibliche astuzie

la sua coscienza... e ironico ardore

liberale... e rozza luce, tra i disgusti

di dandy provinciale, di provinciale

salute... Fino alle infime minuzie

in cui sfumano, nel fondo animale,

Autorità e Anarchia... Ben protetto

dall'impura virtù e dall'ebbro peccare,

difendendo una ingenuità di ossesso,

e con quale coscienza!, vive l'io: io,

vivo, eludendo la vita, con nel petto

The internal and external actions
that flesh him out into existence
are not immune from any of the religions

that are rooted in life, pledges of death,
instituted to cheat
light, to dress lies in light.

His remains: destined to be buried at
Verano, yet his fight with them is Catholic;
the foibles with which he steers his heart

are Jesuitic; his conscience, deep inside,
has biblical cunning . . . and ironic
liberal fervor . . .

and crude light, in the midst of disgust
of a provincial dandy, a provincial
well-being . . . Down to the pettiest minutiae

where Authority and Anarchy, in a beastly
background, lose shape . . . Well sheltered
from impure virtue and wild sinning,

defending a madman's naïveté—
with such awareness!—the self lives: *I* live,
eluding life, with, in my breast,

il senso di una vita che sia oblio

accorante, violento... Ah come

capisco, muto nel fradicio brusio

del vento, qui dov'è muta Roma,

tra i cipressi stancamente sconvolti,

presso te, l'anima il cui graffito suona

Shelley... Come capisco il vortice

dei sentimenti, il capriccio (greco

nel cuore del patrizio, nordico

villeggiante) che lo inghiottì nel cieco

celeste del Tirreno; la carnale

gioia dell'avventura, estetica

e puerile: mentre prostrata l'Italia

come dentro il ventre di un'enorme

cicala, spalanca bianchi litorali,

sparsi nel Lazio di velate torme

di pini, barocchi, di giallognole

radure di ruchetta, dove dorme

col membro gonfio tra gli stracci un sogno

goethiano, il giovincello ciociaro...

Nella Maremma, scuri, di stupende fogne

the sense of a life that may be violent,

rending oblivion . . . How well I understand it,

mute in the drenched sough of the wind,

here where Rome rests without a word, among

the tiredly unsettled cypress trees,

near you, the soul whose inscription calls out

Shelley . . . How well I understand

the maelstrom of feelings, the whim that

(Greek in the heart of the northern patrician

vacationer) swallowed him in the blind

blue of the Tyrrhenian; the carnal ecstasy

of adventure, aesthetic and puerile:

while a prostrated Italy opens wide

—as if inside the belly of an enormous

cicada—niveous beaches, constellated

with misty throngs of baroque pines in Latium,

glades of yellow arugula

where, with his member swollen in his rags,

the young Ciociaro[1]—a dream

from Goethe—sleeps . . .

In the Maremma,[2] dark, with wondrous bogs

---

[1] Ciociaro: a young man from Ciociaria, a commune of Latium

[2] Maremma: a Tuscan-Latial zone along the Tyrrhenian Sea

d'erbasaetta in cui si stampa chiaro

il nocciòlo, pei viottoli che il buttero

della sua gioventù ricolma ignaro.

Ciecamente fragranti nelle asciutte

curve della Versilia, che sul mare

aggrovigliato, cieco, i tersi stucchi,

le tarsie lievi della sua pasquale

campagna interamente umana,

espone, incupita sul Cinquale,

dipanata sotto le torride Apuane,

i blu vitrei sul rosa... Di scogli,

frane, sconvolti, come per un panico

di fragranza, nella Riviera, molle,

erta, dove il sole lotta con la brezza

a dar suprema soavità agli olii

del mare... E intorno ronza di lietezza

lo sterminato strumento a percussione

del sesso e della luce: così avvezza

ne è l'Italia che non ne trema, come

morta nella sua vita: gridano caldi

da centinaia di porti il nome

of spear grass in which hazelnuts
are clearly etched, on paths that the cowhand,
unaware, invests with freshness.

Dizzily fragrant in the dry
curves of Versilia,[3] that on the tangled, blind
sea displays the terse stuccos,

the light inlaying of its paschal
countryside, wholly human,
blackened on the Cinquale,

unraveled under the torrid Apuane,[4]
blues vitreous on the pink . . . Turned upside down
by reefs, landslides, as if by a turmoil

of essences, in the Riviera,[5] soft,
steep, where the sun fights with the breeze
to give utmost suavity

to the sea's calm . . . And all around the boundless
percussion instrument of sex and light hums
merrily: Italy's so used to it

that she is not afraid, numb in its life:
hot from hundreds of ports
the sweating youths,

---

[3] Versilia: area in Tuscany near Maremma
[4] Apuane: Tuscan Apennines
[5] Riviera: Ligurian coastline

del compagno i giovinetti madidi

nel bruno della faccia, tra la gente

rivierasca, presso orti di cardi,

in luride spiaggette...

Mi chiederai tu, morto disadorno,

d'abbandonare questa disperata

passione di essere nel mondo?

6

Me ne vado, ti lascio nella sera

che, benché triste, così dolce scende

per noi viventi, con la luce cerea

che al quartiere in penombra si rapprende.

E lo sommuove. Lo fa più grande, vuoto,

intorno, e, più lontano, lo riaccende

di una vita smaniosa che del roco

rotolio dei tram, dei gridi umani,

dialettali, fa un concerto fioco

e assoluto. E senti come in quei lontani

esseri che, in vita, gridano, ridono,

in quei loro veicoli, in quei grami

caseggiati dove si consuma l'infido

ed espansivo dono dell'esistenza—

quella vita non è che un brivido;

with dark faces, among
fishermen, patches of cardoon,
on sooty little beaches

scream the name of their pals . . .

Will you, who died so simply,
ask me to quench this desperate
itch to be in the world?

6

I am going, I leave you in the evening
that, although sad, descends so mildly
for us, the living, with the waxen light

that mingles with the dusky quarter
and stirs it, makes it bigger, empty all around,
and farther out it kindles it again

‚with a frenetic life that makes
a feeble, absolute concerto
out of a raucous rolling

of trolleys, human screams
in dialect. And you feel how in those
far beings who in life yell, laugh, in their

vehicles, in those sordid tenements
where the tricky and glib gift of existence
is accomplished—that life's only a cheap thrill;

corporea, collettiva presenza;

senti il mancare di ogni religione

vera; non vita, ma sopravvivenza

—forse più lieta della vita—come

d'un popolo di animali, nel cui arcano

orgasmo non ci sia altra passione

che per l'operare quotidiano:

umile fervore cui dà un senso di festa

l'umile corruzione. Quanto più è vano

—in questo vuoto della storia, in questa

ronzante pausa in cui la vita tace—

ogni ideale, meglio è manifesta

la stupenda, adusta sensualità

quasi alessandrina, che tutto minia

e impuramente accende, quando qua

nel mondo, qualcosa crolla, e si trascina

il mondo, nella penombra, rientrando

in vuote piazze, in scorate officine...

Già si accendono i lumi, costellando

Via Zabaglia, Via Franklin, l'intero

Testaccio, disadorno tra il suo grande

earthy, collective presence;

you feel the lack of any true religion,

not life, but mere survival—

perhaps more jubilant than life—

as of a bunch of animals,

in whose arcane orgasm there's no passion

other than daily chores:

a humble zeal to which humble corruption

gives festiveness. In this vacuum of history,

this ticking pause where life is mute,

how truly vain is every ideal, how better

shines the marvelous, sunburnt sensuality,

almost Alexandrine, that limns

and lewdly ignites all things

when here on earth some parts

crumble and in the twilight

the world drags itself back

to empty squares, glum factories . . .

Already lights come on, spangling Zabaglia

Street, Franklin Street, all of Testaccio, bare

between its huge, polluted hill, the banks

lurido monte, i lungoteveri, il nero
fondale, oltre il fiume, che Monteverde
ammassa o sfuma invisibile sul cielo.

Diademi di luci che si perdono,
smaglianti, e freddi di tristezza
quasi marina... Manca poco alla cena;

brillano i rari autobus del quartiere,
con grappoli d'operai agli sportelli,
e gruppi di militari vanno, senza fretta,

verso il monte che cela in mezzo a sterri
fradici e mucchi secchi d'immondizia
nell'ombra, rintanate zoccolette

che aspettano irose sopra la sporcizia
afrodisiaca: e, non lontano, tra casette
abusive ai margini del monte, o in mezzo

a palazzi, quasi a mondi, dei ragazzi
leggeri come stracci giocano alla brezza
non più fredda, primaverile; ardenti

di sventatezza giovanile la romanesca
loro sera di maggio scuri adolescenti
fischiano pei marciapiedi, nella festa

of the Tiber, the black backdrop beyond
the river that Monteverde amasses
or melts invisibly in the sky.

Diadems of light that vanish, brilliant,
and cold with a close to sealike sadness . . .
Supper is almost ready, and the rare

neighborhood buses shine
with clusters of workers at the windows,
and soldiers bunched together calmly stomp

toward the mountain that hides,
in soggy excavations and dry mounds
of garbage, little sluts laired in the shadow

spitefully waiting atop the aphrodisiac
mess: and, not far, among the squatters' homes
on the rim of the mountain, or amidst

palaces, to them worlds, some boys as light
as rags play in the breeze of spring
no longer cold; impetuous

with youthful wildness brown-skinned adolescents
on streets catcall their Roman May
eve, in the vespers' idyll;

vespertina; e scrosciano le saracinesche

dei garages di schianto, gioiosamente,

se il buio ha resa serena la sera,

e in mezzo ai platani di Piazza Testaccio

il vento che cade in tremiti di bufera,

è ben dolce, benché radendo i capellacci

e i tufi del Macello, vi si imbeva

di sangue marcio, e per ogni dove

agiti rifiuti e odore di miseria.

È un brusio la vita, e questi persi

in essa, la perdono serenamente,

se il cuore ne hanno pieno: a godersi

eccoli, miseri, la sera: e potente

in essi, inermi, per essi, il mito

rinasce... Ma io, con il cuore cosciente

di chi soltanto nella storia ha vita,

potrò mai più con pura passione operare,

se so che la nostra storia è finita?

down crash the rolling shutters of garages,

happily if the dark has made the evening

serene, and through the plane trees of Testaccio.

Square the wind that is falling

with stormy shivers is quite sweet,

even if as it grazes long-haired youths

and the Slaughterhouse tufa, it soaks up

putrid blood, wafting garbage

and stench of misery everywhere.

Life is a beehive, and these who are lost in it,

lose it at peace, if their

heart is full: there they go,

to enjoy, poor folks, the evening: and through them,

powerless, the myth is powerfully reborn . . .

But I, with the cognizant heart of one

who lives only in history, will I

ever be able to exert my pure passion

since I know that our story is done?

ALFREDO DE PALCHI

Alfredo de Palchi was born in Verona in 1926 and raised by his anarchist grandfather after his father abandoned him. A staunch antifascist, de Palchi refused to conform under Mussolini and was imprisoned and tortured by the Fascists during World War II in Legnano, near Verona. After the war, he rejected military service and was imprisoned for six years in Naples, where he began writing verse. On his release from prison, he served (unwillingly) in the military until he was classified as unstable and discharged. In 1956, after traveling around Europe, he moved to New York City, where he worked as a translator and editor of the literary review *Chelsea* and where he lives today. De Palchi published his first collection of poetry, *Sessioni con l'analista* ("Sessions with My Analyst"), in 1970, which was followed by several collections, including *Le viziose avversioni* (1999; "Addictive Aversions") and *Paradigma* (2001; "Paradigm"). An Italian living in America for more than forty years, he writes from a position of exile, a sentiment clear in "Quanto usufruire dello spasimo" ("So Much Fruition of Spasms"), where "la distanza uccide" ("distance kills"). His verse has two central tropes: intense despair and sexual abandon.

Orecchio il silenzio...

Orecchio il silenzio di quella sedia

con la mattina cigolante di gabbiani attorno la guglia,

e già il passo delle tribù

occupa tanto spazio tra i muri di questo deposito

abissale di spiriti e di pietra calcarea

dove in ginocchio dal peso delle colpe

ti divoro la verticale spogliazione di Barbara

con l'intento di uscirne illeso

alleggerito dalla benedizione del portale.

Che significato incontra la mia casa desertica di ossa

travolta da malignità occulte

e che mentre vi cala dentro si macera di tremori

per l'abisso lucido della triangolazione—

incontro il tuo viso di perpetua, illuminante

perch'io possa significarmi nel rito

della simbologia carnale.

È dubbia la sicurezza di fronte a tanta omertà—

il caleidoscopio sonoro tra le pietre

e le vetrate che illustrano donne biblicamente erotiche

assicura che il compimento fruibile è perfetto nella fossa,

Barbara di muschi...

Grace Church, New York City, novembre 1999

I catch the silence...

I catch the silence of that chair
with morning squeaking with gulls around the spire;
already trekking tribes
take up so much room among the walls
of this abysmal warehouse
of ghosts, calcareous stone
where on my knees for weight of sins I eat
Barbara's vertical undressing
thinking of getting out unharmed
and shriven by the portal's benediction.

What meaning does my house bleached like a bone
swept away by occult malignancies
uncover—which as it dives into that gloom
tortures itself with tremblings
for the lucid abyss of triangulation—
and then I see your face, a vestal's,
dispensing light so that I may find purpose
in the ritual of carnal archetype.

Safety is at risk, challenged with wrong integrity—
kaleidoscope sonorous among stones
and stained-glass windows framing women biblically
erotic reinforces that a fruitful
consummation is perfect in the grave,
Barbara of mosses . . .

Grace Church, New York City, November 1999

Sono il dilemma...

Sono il dilemma
che oltraggia la veste monacale usata dalla mente,
e per il tuo corpo incolume
sono lo Sposo della mensa
adorato ogni notte in ginocchio presso
il letto spogliato quanto te;
la veste intatta ad un chiodo a poco a poco si chiazza
di unguenti spalmati sulle piaghe dell'intimo punire
mentre tenti di fermare la mano surreale che ti accende
e ti invischia nella sua potenza.
La finestra della cella è chiusa, l'uscio sbarrato,
i muri calcinati assorbono le urla mute;
e tu, monacale, divarichi le carni ustionate,
e con la bocca saturnina piena di lingua che serpeggia lucifera
avvolgi nell'ideare il mio Calvario infiammato
vinto con la religione della tua essenza
carnale—prendimi come vuoi,
in tutte le tue bocche gonfie di rosa, turgide di Passione,
rièmpiti del tuo Salvatore.

4 febbraio 2000

I am the quandary disgracing...

I am the quandary disgracing
the priestly cassock employed by the mind,
and for your intact body
I am the banquet's Groom
worshiped each night on knees
by the bed naked as you are;
the flawless robe off a hook is slowly dappled
by unguents rubbed on sores of inner scourging
· while you try to stop the unreal hand
that kindles and inveigles you in its power.
The cell's window is closed, the door is barred,
the mortared walls absorb the muted screams;
nunlike you part the sizzled flesh
and with saturnine mouth full of satanic
snake-tongue you wind in your imagining
my flaming Calvary won over by the cult
of your fleshy quintessence—
take me as you like, in all your pink-fraught mouths,
turgid with Passion, fill
yourself with your Savior.

4 February 2000

Quanto usufruire dello spasimo...

Quanto usufruire dello spasimo che ci scuote,

e le mani si cercano nelle nebbie

sotterranee di fili di voci travolgenti,

che mi spinge a te vedova nera di un evento

che tormenta nelle braccia il tormento

quando si è soli nelle proprie braccia.

Guardami, dimmi, è così per te, trafissa nell'astruso

esplodere di parole vocali insensate,

udite con tenerezza mentre ciascuno percepisce

penetrando l'immagine che l'una ha dell'altro,

e generate nel tuo terreno seminabile a onde assiderato

con fioriture sotto una coltre di polvere;

io sono chi tu cerchi, sono

il giogo felice che trovi per le colline infertili,

le miniere di sale, le pianure e le vie disertate

che stringono il domicilio semispento;

parlami col tuo sesso alla gola,

urlami dentro che sei chi mi offre il proprio terreno

vivacemente di acque colline pianure e foreste chiare;

tu sai, la distanza uccide.

5 febbraio 2000

So much fruition of spasms...

So much fruition of spasms that shake us,
hands looking for each other
'in subterranean fogs of sweeping whispers.
It drives me to you, black widow of an event
that wounds in the arms the torment
when we are alone in our own arms.
Look at me, tell me it is the same for you,
transfixed in the abstruse
explosion of insensate words and vowels—
absorbed with tenderness while each
perceives, piercing, the image
that one has of the other—
hatched in your plot in germinating waves
frozen in bloom under a pall of dust;
I am the one you're looking for,
I am the happy yoke you find for barren hills,
salt mines, the plains and the deserted streets
hugging the lukewarm home;
speak to me with your sex at my throat,
holler inside that you're the one
who offers me her ground
lively with waters hills plains and clear forests;
you know how distance kills.

5 February 2000

Amelia Rosselli

Amelia Rosselli, one of the best-known Italian poets, was born in Paris in 1930. Her life and work are characterized by continual displacement. After her father, Carlo, and brother, Nello, were murdered by Mussolini's henchmen in 1937 (both were politically active antifascists), the family moved to England (Rosselli's mother, Marion Cave, was English) and then fled to the United States to wait out the war. Rosselli returned to Europe in 1946, living in England, where she studied literature and music (a great love throughout her life). She returned to Rome in 1948. The deaths of her mother and grandmother were followed by the death of her close friend, the poet Rocco Scotellaro, in 1953. She supported herself as a translator. She developed symptoms of mental illness and for the rest of her life suffered breakdowns and extended stays in mental hospitals. Rosselli published her first collection of poetry, *Variazioni belliche* ("War Variations"), in 1964 to critical acclaim. Her other collections are *Serie ospedaliera* (1969; "Hospital Series"), *Impromptu* (1981), and *Sleep: Poesie in inglese* (1992; "Sleep: Poems in English"). She committed suicide in Rome in 1996. Multilingualism, music, and psychoanalysis are important themes in her highly experimental verse.

Lo sdrucciolo cuore...

Lo sdrucciolo cuore che in me è ribelle
quasi sempre in me preferirebbe
una più saggia angoscia
l'animo è davvero poca cosa
è davvero
infernale così come tu dici.

Ma credevo nel soldo e nella miseria
assieme assetati di vendetta: o credevo
nel lento pellegrinaggio ad una fonte
dedicata ad un pubblico e anche privatissimo
dibattito, che essa ingigantisce
così ingegnosa.

Nessuna fede ha mai mosso le montagne
tu muovi le montagne in me, tu che sei
compagno di un momento e senza amore
con quel tuo chiarore di corta vita
l'estate stessa spiovente
nel suo abracadabra di giovinezza irresponsabile
ricevo dalle tue abbondanti e magrissime braccia.

The dactylic heart...

The dactylic heart that in me is a rebel
almost always prefers to see in me
a wiser anguish
the mind is really a trifle
really hellish as you say.

But I believed in dough and poverty
together thirsty for revenge: or I
believed in the slow pilgrimage to a spring
dedicated to a public and also very
private debate, that it
so wittily blows up.

No faith ever moved mountains
you move mountains in me, you who are a casual
and loveless friend
with your short-lived flamboyance
summer itself cascading
in its mumbo jumbo of irresponsible youth
I receive from your plentiful
and sticklike arms.

Mio angelo, io non seppi mai...

Mio angelo, io non seppi mai quale angelo
fosti, o per quali vie storte ti amai
o venerai, tu che scendendo ogni gradino
sembravi salirli, frustarmi, mostrarmi
una vita tutta perduta alla ragione, quando
facesti al caso quel che esso riprometteva,
cioè mi lasciasti.

Non seppi nemmeno perché tra tanti chiarori
eccitati dell'intelletto in pena, vi
furono così sotterranee evoluzioni d'un
accordarsi al mio, al vostro e tuo bisogno
d'una sterilità completa.

Eppure eccomi qua, a scrivere versi,
come se fosse non del tutto astratto
alla mia ricerca d'un enciclopedico
capire quasi tutto a me offerto senza
lo spazio d'una volontà di ferro a controllare
quel poco del tutto così mal offerto.

My angel, I never knew...

My angel, I never knew what kind of angel
you were, or by what devious ways I loved you
or worshiped you, who coming down each step
appeared to climb them, to torture me, to show me
a life completely lost to reason, when you did
with chance what it intended
should be done, and you left me.

I also didn't know why with so many
excited flashes of the mind in pain, there were
such subterranean stages to be agreed on
with mine, your friends' and your
need of utter sterility.

And yet here I am, writing poetry,
as if it were not totally extraneous
to my encyclopedic search
to understand almost everything offered me
without room for an iron will to check
that little of the all so poorly offered.

The Neo-Avant-Garde

ALFREDO GIULIANI

Born in Monbaroccio, near Pesaro, in 1924, Alfredo Giuliani is one of the most active members of the new Italian avant-garde. He has a degree in philosophy from the University of Rome. He currently resides in Rome and has worked as an editor, journalist (contributing regularly to *La repubblica*), critic, translator (of James Joyce and Dylan Thomas, among others), visual artist, and poet. He was a founding member of the experimental Gruppo 63 and edited the influential *I novissimi: Poesie per gli anni '60* (1961; "The Newest Poets: Poetry for the Sixties"), whose intent was to rupture traditional linguistic structures. His first collection of poetry, *Il cuore zoppo* ("The Crippled Heart"), was published in 1955 and followed by *Povera Juliet e altre poesie* (1965; " 'Poor Juliet' and Other Poems") and *Ebbrezza di placamenti* (1993; "The Joy of Placation"). He has taught Italian literature at the University of Bologna and Chieti and has been a visiting professor at New York University. Essentially a Marxist, he manipulates and plays with language to criticize contemporary social, political, and economic ills—"Prologo" ("Prologue") is an example. He is also interested in the connection between psychoanalysis and writing.

I giorni aggrappati alla città...

I giorni aggrappati alla città e diseredati,
la vuota fornace ribrucia scorie morte.

Tortuoso di scatti e abbandoni, il polso feroce
misura l'orologio di sabbia, le orme ineguali
dell'ansia. Lo scrimolo del mare, oltre di me
nel mio canto si sporge.

Segreto è il lavoro che a farmi l'occhio sereno
nomina il mare distante. Nessun amico può dirmi
menzogne ch'io non conosca, nessuna donna
oltrepassare il suo messaggio di lode o di resa.

Io vedo le mie parole,
le mie terre brucate dal silenzio mortale, schierarsi
lungo l'ultima ora del giorno tormentato di vele,
e rievocarmi.

Days dispossessed...

Days dispossessed and clinging to the city.
The empty furnace rekindles dead dross.
Tortuous with fits and starts, the wild beat marks
the sandglass and the uneven
footprints of tension. I surpass
the ocean's limit in my song.

Secret's the work that names the distant sea
to make my vision clear. No friend can tell me
lies I don't know, no woman go beyond
her message of love or surrender.

                    I see my words,
my lands grazed by death's silence gather around
the sail-torn day's last hour
and resurrect me.

This poem was written in 1951 or 1952.

Il mondo è gremito di voci

Odi che il violino mendico s'arrampica

su per una chiocciola di note

dietro il muro tarlato della pergola,

sa di furto e di pece lo sghembo suono.

Lèbile il vento il cuore delle corde

propaga alle tue parole, le mie trasale

di silenzio e di gridi.

Questa luna

che bucolica molce l'erba autunnale

guida le tue maree

scande gli esametri del mare.

Il mondo è gremito di voci, gloriose

o reiette o dolorose,

che tutte seconda un richiamo;

e a me la più cara che dice:

Tu non mi ami quanto io ti amo.

The World's Crowded with Voices

Hear the beggar viola reaching up
a stairway of notes behind the gnawed wall of the arbor:
its slanted sound feels like larceny and pitch.

A tenuous wind propagates to your words
the heart of strings, scares mine
with silence and loud cries.
                    This pastoral
moon that caresses the autumnal grass
leads your tides, scans the meters of the sea.

This world is crowded with astounding, vile,
dolorous voices, all following a cue;
to me the dearest says you don't love me
as much as I love you.

Nel mio cieco parlare,...

Nel mio cieco parlare, nel buio racconto

dello sparviero occhio il mio lume fugace,

gioia del fuco, del flutto che onda e dispare

e della pietra fluviale lambita sul greto,

dell'albero lavoro segreto,

di conchiglia rombo stellare.

Arde la mia città come un cespuglio,

tutte le mie bocche hanno sete. E prego

acqualuce pei teneri germogli della voce,

per la muta oscura polvere che i giorni discarna;

usura e amore. E il silenzio mi brucia.

In my blind speech,...

In my blind speech, in the dark tale
of eagle eyes my fleeting light,
joy of the drone, of waves surging and down
tumbling, the fluvial stone
laved on the shore, secret work of a tree,
star vortex in a shell.

My city flares like Horeb, all my mouths
are thirsty. I pray waterlight for the tender
buds of my speech, for the dark dust that eats
at each day—usury and love. And silence burns me.

EDOARDO SANGUINETI

Edoardo Sanguineti, a founding member of Gruppo 63, was born in 1930 in Genoa, where he later taught Italian literature at the university. He studied in Turin and went on to teach in Salerno. Like Giuliani, he is a seminal figure in the Italian neo-avant-garde. He contributed to the experimental poetry anthology *I novissimi: Poesia per gli anni '60* and has taken part in the cultural life of Italy as a poet, translator, critic, novelist, editor, librettist, politician, and playwright. His first volume of verse, *Laborintus*, was published in 1956 and followed by many collections of poetry, including *Erotopaegnia* (1960), *Wirrwarr* (1972), and *Corollario* (1997; "Corollary"). In 1969 he edited the influential poetry anthology *Poesia italiana del Novecento* ("Twentieth-Century Italian Poetry"). A decidedly political man, he contributed to many left-wing journals and newspapers, such as *Paese sera* and *L'unità*; served on the Genoese city council; and was a member of Parliament, representing the Communist Party from 1979 to 1983. Narrative displacement and multilingualism are common in his poetry (he was influenced by Ezra Pound), and the reader is frequently left feeling alienated from a poem's theme (be it political, erotic, or social). Narrative estrangement can have a political function, as the poet lays bare the idiosyncrasies and contradictions of bourgeois culture.

Erotopaegnia 7

la cosa come la passa; (la porta appunto); (la coscia); (la
    finestretta): il pugnale!
(la passa!); e tremando! (proporzioni terribili!);
    ingigantito! premendo(...);
e la bottiglia appunto:
    nelle latrine; e così appunto; in quell'aria
infetta; lei paziente, bianchissima: e come la passa questo
    pugnale! tremando!

Erotopaegnia 7

how it presses into her;[1] (the door, just so); (the thigh);

      (the little window): the knife!

(it presses into her!) and quivering! (dreadful dimensions!);

      (overblown! pushing . . .);

and the bottle just so:

   in the toilets; and that's it just so; in that

foul air; she patient, stark white: and how his knife presses

      into her! quivering!

---

[1] From the philosopher Giordano Bruno's *Dinner of Ashes*

Erotopaegnia 9

e oltre la porta a vetri, l'improvvisa piscina;[1] e lei, e

nella nebbia,

una volta ancora, e perduta!

osservavo infatti (e da una di quelle finestrette)

la piazza deserta, i palazzi deformi, crollanti: ancora

ascoltavo, ancora

quel silenzio; e quell'aria odoravo, e immobile; e io stesso

infatti,

e perduto, ancora; ma oltre i vetri vedi grigiastra

l'acqua; vedi

i viluppi di vibrati, di arsi nudi, e ancora:

ancora il pulito

fiato di lei desiderando; e io stesso, allora, e in quell'acqua,

miseramente,

e perduto; e la gola di lei, e ancora, e la pulita, di lei,

allora, gola!

dall'acqua, e in un singulto, quegli iracondi, immensi,

oscillando, nudi!

tiepido, oh tiepido coro, oh molle, toccando, coro, ciò che

nominavano;

---

[1] La scena d'inferno si è ora spostata in una irreale piscina accademica. La nebbia grava sulla città, vista attraverso i vetri di una finestra, e penetra nell'edificio. La piscina è colma di esseri nudi, gli studenti, che si toccano e ostentano i testicoli. Tutto appare deforme e corrotto; nel grosso «ventre» della piscina gli studenti conducono i loro giochi omosessuali. Verso la fine la visione della donna «innescata» e «pressa» nella bolgia erotica. [Sanguineti's note]

Erotopaegnia 9

and beyond the glass door, the unexpected pool;[1] and she,

 and in the fog,

one more time, and lost!

 I was watching in fact (and from one little window)

the deserted square, the misshapen, crumbling palaces: I was

 still listening, that

silence still; and I smelled that air, and fixed; and I

 myself indeed,

and lost, still; but beyond the glass you see grayish water;

 you see

tangles of shaken ones, of burning naked ones, and still:

 still wanting her

clean breath: and I myself, then, and in that water,

 pitifully,

and lost; and her throat, and still, and the clean, then,

 throat of hers!

from out the water, and in a gurgle, those angry people, huge,

 swaying, naked!

tepid, oh tepid chorus, oh soft, touching, chorus,

 what they named;

---

[1] The infernal scene now moves to a surrealistic, academic pool. From a window, one sees thick fog blanketing the city, seeping into the building. The pool is filled with naked students touching themselves and flaunting their sex. Everything looks corrupt and twisted; in the big "belly" of the pool, the students enact homosexual games. Toward the end we see the "hooked" and "pressed" woman in the erotic cauldron. [Sanguineti's note]

coro, ancora: testibus (esplosivi gridando)! testibus

(deformi toccando)!

testibus (deformi testes!)! et praesentibus, oh!

e penetrava la caligine;

e lucidissima; e vibrante, allora, ardente, l'acqua; e in

calde coppe,

copulati; in sridenti vasche, voltolati; urlando,

bollenti:

in questo ventre (così allora urlando!) premendo! pressi,

allora, gemendo;

colando, impressi: oh, frangibili (dissi);

e vidi lei, innescata, grondando, oh!

(praesentibus testibus vidi); lei vibrata vidi; vibrante;

lei appunto;

pressa.

chorus, still: testibus (about to explode screaming)! testibus

(deformed ones touching)!

testibus (misshapen testes!)! et praesentibus, oh!

and the haze rolling in;

and very bright; and pulsing, then, burning, the water;

and in hot bowls,

coupled; in shrieking tubs, turned; screaming, boiling:

in this belly (this way then screaming!) pressing! pressed, then

moaning;

dripping, crushed: oh you, who can be shattered (I said);

and saw her, hooked, dripping, oh!

(praesentibus testibus I saw);[2] shaken I saw; shaking;

her just so;

pressed.

---

[2] "With attending witnesses"

Contemporary Poets

Anna Malfaiera

Born in Fabriano in 1926, Anna Malfaiera studied at the University of Urbino and then moved to Rome, where she worked as a teacher. She published her first poems in the anthology *Letteratura* ("Literature") when she was just twenty. Her first collection, *Fermo davanzale* ("Firm Windowsill"), appeared in 1961 and was followed by *Il vantaggio privato* (1967; "Private Advantage"), *Verso l'imperfetto* (1984; "Toward the Imperfect"), and *Il più considerevole* (1993; "The Most Considerable"), among others. Between 1987 and 1989, she worked in theater, with the Progetto Fabula, and two of her productions were staged in Rome. She died in her hometown in 1996. Her earlier verse addresses many of the technical and thematic concerns of the poems of the group of writers known as the Novissimi (experimentation with language, lack of punctuation), while her later and more philosophical writings, such as *Lo stato d'emergenza* (1971; "State of Emergency"), are socially engaged. Her "state of emergency" specifically evokes the *anni di piombo* ("leaden years"), the volatile and violent period of terrorism, strikes, and protests of the late 1960s and 1970s.

Ho spesso un senso malsano...

Ho spesso un senso malsano di rinuncia

e quello d'intristire quanto di più amavo

senza benevolenza gli anni annegati

senza turbamento. Per me volere o non volere

è un'astensione che dentro mi dissecca.

A chi dirò a chi meglio potrò a chi mai

mai dove quanto dire quando e perché

l'urgenza del dire non ha mai fine.

Siamo al grado zero...

Siamo al grado zero di valenze perdute

un inventario di complicità casuali e no

di assurdità credibili. Campionario.

Furbi cretini porci scemi. E l'orco?

e gli sciacalli? e i coglioni? Ahi!

Faccia a faccia insultandoci corpo

a corpo scontrandoci persiste accanita

la volontà irriducibile del sopraffarci.

I often have an unhealthy sense...

I often have an unhealthy sense of renunciation
and of saddening what I loved most
without benevolence the drowned years
without perturbation. To me wanting or not wanting
is an abstention that dries me up inside.
To whom will I tell to whom will I best be able
to whom ever where how much tell when and why
the urge to tell never ends.

We are at zero level...

We are at zero level of lost valencies
an inventory of happenstance complicities
of credible absurdities. A sample.
Smartalecks cretins pigs idiots. And the bogeyman?
and the jackals? and the balls? Ouch!
Face to face insulting each other
in hand-to-hand combat
the relentless will to squash each other
irreducibly persists.

Luigi Fontanella

Luigi Fontanella was born in 1943 in San Severino, near Salerno. He completed his degree in Italian literature at the University of Rome and received a PhD in Romance languages and literatures from Harvard. After two years as a Fulbright fellow at Princeton University, he became a professor of Italian in the Department of European Languages, Literatures, and Cultures at Stony Brook, where he still teaches and edits *Gradiva*, an international journal of Italian poetry. His first collection, *La verifica incerta* (1972; "The Unsure Verification"), was followed by *La vita trasparente* (1978; "The Transparent Life"), *Round Trip* (1991), and *Ceres* (1996). His poems appear in many American and Italian anthologies. He has also written plays, short stories, and novels and has worked extensively as a critic and translator. Displacement, both physical and narrative, is a common theme in his work, and many of his poems chronicle his frequent journeys between the United States and Italy. Fontanella experiments with language, and multilingualism, minimal punctuation, and neologisms are common in his poetry.

Quattro barche di pescatori...

Quattro barche di pescatori
su di un mare lattiginoso:
stenta qui la memoria a coniugare

queste immagini di repertorio
alle riaffermate urgenze dell'oggi
io disertore spento che di passaggio

(sempre di passaggio) trasferisco
duri segni di aggiornati retaggi
in immagini di vita riflessa:

è buono questo mare
è buona questa terra
per tutti i suoi figli eletti e reietti.

Napoli-Salerno, marzo 1991

Four fishermen's boats...

Four fishermen's boats
on a milky sea:
memory struggles here

to marry these stock images
to the resurfacing urgency of the now
me a worn-out deserter that in passing

(always in passing) metamorphoses
hard signs of present legacies
into depictions of reflected life:

this sea is good
this land is good
for all its elect and cast-out sons.

Naples-Salerno, March 1991

Quando ad un tratto...

Quando ad un tratto si fa strada in luce
virginiana tra false pastorali e soavità
di visi ignoti. Stanotte ronzava

perfetta in forma e sequenza. Che restasse
accanto n'ero certo, ma svanita è già
stamattina. Ricercarne ora il contorno

la figura, l'ombra, una marginale
rassomiglianza, almeno quella folgore
iniziale, una movenza, una parola sola,

un niente che riaccenda il perduto sogno
cui ora invano m'inchino. Pesta poesia,
innamorata del tuo manichino.

Charlottesville, aprile 1990–East Setauket, aprile 1992

When all of a sudden...

When all of a sudden it makes headway
in a Virginian light through phony pastorals
and meekness of strange faces. Just tonight

it hummed so perfect in its form and sequence.
Sure, it stayed by me, but this morning already
it was gone. Now look for its contour

its figure, its shadow, a marginal resemblance,
at least that initial bolt of lightning,
a move, a unique word,

a nothing that rekindle the lost dream
I bow to now, in vain. Spoiled poetry
in love with your own dummy.

Charlottesville, April 1990–East Setauket, April 1992

Hegira

Di colpo invaso da una calma apparente
tutto gioca a sfarsi mollemente
in digradante intreccio di colori
comunione di spazi una volta spuntati

non Caino che uccide suo fratello
non orgia di sangue innocente
sprofondo la mia faccia nella terra
senza paura raccolgo il seme

sparso d'un'altra cerimonia:
acqua sono e terra e fronda
al di là di ogni impostura
abbattuto il muro della recitazione

apparenza non è finzione
ma reale connubio di forze
una festa calma che rassicura.
Respiro questo vento

tempo e voci di lontani compagni:
è segno non più sgomento
del mio avvenuto annullamento.
Mi ricorda che a lui dovrò

Hegira

Absorbed all of a sudden
by an apparent calm
everything plays to be peacefully unmade
in a receding web of colors.

Not Cain killing his brother
or orgy of blameless blood:
I shove my face into the earth
fearless I gather the spilled seed

of yet another ritual: I am water
and soil and frond beyond any concoction,
·the wall of acting crushed
apppearance is not fiction

but real merging of strengths
a poised feast that reassures.
I breathe this wind, recall
the time and voices of gone friends:

it is a sign, no longer panic
for my destined downgrading.
It tells me that I'll have
to surrender to him, him whom I dared

consegnarmi, a lui che osavo

sfidare e che non conosce sconfitta

o pentimento. A lui l'improvviso

brivido della sera cui dovrà seguire

la lunga mattina. A lui l'eterna

primavera, lui miscelatore di voci

in una Lingua sola. Messaggero

che viene da lontano e che va lontano

come una grazia ogni volta adempiuta.

Solo *riconoscendomi* in lui

potrò riappropriarmi di ciò

che ho smarrito fin dalla mia venuta.

Monte Porzio, maggio 1991

to challenge, he who does not know defeat
or repentance. To him the scary shudder
of evening followed by slow-burning morning.
To him the eternal spring: he who commingles

voices into One Tongue, messenger coming
from afar, going far, like grace fulfilled.
Only *by finding myself* in him can I
regain what I lost when I first came.

Monte Porzio, May 1991

Milo De Angelis

Milo De Angelis was born in Milan in 1951. He studied at the Universities of Milan and Montpellier and received a degree in Italian literature and classics. Several of De Angelis's poems appeared in anthologies in the mid-1970s. His first collection, *Somiglianze* (1976; "Resemblances"), was followed by *Millimetri* (1983; "Millimeters"), *Distante un padre* (1989; "A Distant Father"), and *Biografia sommaria* (1999; "Abridged Biography"), among others. He worked as a tutor of Greek and Latin in Milan; directed the poetry journal *Niebo*; and is also a novelist, translator of Greek and Latin, and literary critic. He currently lives in Rome. His poetry pushes the boundaries of language, a characteristic that aligns his early verse with the neo-avant-garde. His interest in psychoanalysis and philosophy (in particular Martin Heidegger and Gilles Deleuze) is clear in poems such as "Sala parto" ("Delivery Room").

Sala parto

«Non bere la neve,

la neve è una malattia con piume e stormi,

un moto tra i pianeti, una

lentissima bugia. E noi abbiamo venduto la luce

con due spighe fuoritempo,

abbiamo la morte nelle gambe cieche».

«Ricorda la storia

di Fracido, nel terzo reparto: vide le mani

del chirurgo che non scordò il suo errore,

le mani sulla maniglia del taxi

i vetri pesanti che gelavano,

la corsa violenta».

«Non ti ho mai parlato

di tua madre. Era

bella come l'alga, triste

come i tentacoli dell'aragosta, forte come le

pupille».

Delivery Room

"Don't drink the snow,

the snow is a sickness with feathers and flocks,

a motion among planets, a

very slow lie. And we have sold the light

with two shafts not in season;

we hold death between our blind legs."

"Remember the story

of Fracido, in the third ward: he saw the hands

of the surgeon who did not forget his mistake,

the hands on the handle of the taxi

the heavy glass that frosted,

the wild race."

"I never told you about your mother.

She was as beautiful as algae,

sad as the tentacles of the lobster,

piercing as a glance."

Per quell'innato scatto

Nel superotto girato al ginnasio

è già lei: la ragazza guerriera

sempre all'attacco.

Faceva segnali di fumo, fuochi di bivacco,

gettava in pattumiera i profumi ottocenteschi.

Ragazza dei baratri e dei bar, dei giochi

di destrezza, dei campionati studenteschi

vinti in scioltezza: nove secondi

con sei metri di distacco.

E io, in classe, quando mi accorsi che volava

(«Nove netti sugli ottanta,

a quindici anni, ragazzi!»)

l'ho chiamata subito Atalanta.

Stefania Annovazzi

si chiamava veramente

più spesso Stefanella.

Ma per tutti noi era quella

divina falcata adolescente.

For That Innate Dash

In the 8mm film shown at the gymnasium

it's already she: the warrior girl

always on the attack.

She made smoke signals, bivouac fires,

throwing romantic perfumes in the garbage can.

Girl of dives and bars, of games of

skill, easy winner of the student

championships: nine seconds

and six meters ahead.

And I, in class, becoming aware she was flying

("Nine clear on the eighty

at the age of fifteen, guys!"),

quickly dubbed her Atalanta.

Stefania Annovazzi

was really more

often called Stefanella.

But for all of us she was that

divine adolescent dash.

Semifinale

La Doxa mi chiede per chi voterò. La voce

è di un ragazzo che, dall'altra parte, respira. Non so

quale chiarezza dentro la rovina. Tutto

ritorna qui, confine del luogo. Quel non parlato

di chiodi per terra. Il Professor D'Amato spiegava

un pronome... *nemo*: nessuno, *non nemo*: qualcuno.

Nessuno giungerà oltre le vene, è semplice, ragazzi.

    Qualcuno

è scomparso o comunque non dà notizie. Il postino

mi consiglia di guardare meglio nella buca,

anche in quelle vicine. Guarderò. *Neminem*

excipi diem: per nessun giorno ho fatto eccezione.

Morire è dunque perdere anche la morte, infinito

presente, nessun appello, nessuna musica

di una chiamata personale. Oltre le vene che furono rito

e dimora, milligrammo e annuncio, grido infinito

di gioia o di soccorso, nessuno mai

oltre queste vene. È semplice, ragazzi, nessuno.

Semifinal

The pollster asks who I will vote for. The voice
is a boy's that breathes from the other side. I don't know
what clarity from the ruin. All comes back here,
to its limit. Nails on the ground, mute.
Professor D'Amato explained
a pronoun . . . *nemo*: no one, *non nemo*: someone.
No one will reach beyond the pulse, it's simple, boys.

    Someone
has disappeared or anyway gives no news. The postman
advises me to look into the mailbox more carefully,
even in those nearby. I will look. *Neminem*
excipi diem: I made no exception on any day.
Dying is then losing even death, infinite
present, no appeal, no music
of a personal call. Beyond the pulse that was rite
and residence, milligram and announcement, infinite cry
of joy or help, no one ever
beyond this pulse. It's simple, boys, no one.

VALERIO MAGRELLI

Valerio Magrelli was born in Rome in 1957. He studied at the Sorbonne (literature and film) and earned a degree in philosophy from the University of Rome. In the late 1970s he began publishing his poetry in literary journals, including *Nuovi argomenti* ("New Topics"). His first collected volume, *Ora serrata retinae* ("The Jagged Border of the Eye"), came out in 1980 and won the Premio Mondello. His second collection, *Nature e venature* (1987; "Essences and Imprints"), was followed by *Esercizi di tipologia* (1992; "Typology Exercises") and *Didascalie per la lettura di un giornale* (1999; "Instructions for Reading the Newspaper"). Magrelli also works as a translator, journalist, and literary critic and currently teaches French language and literature at the University of Pisa. His concerns—intertextuality, the act of reading, everyday happenings—take the form of clear, rational verse. He is keenly interested in the act of looking: words such as *occhio* ("eye"), *distinguere* ("to distinguish"), and *sguardo* ("a look or glance") are common.

Ogni sera chino sul chiaro...

Ogni sera chino sul chiaro
orto delle pagine,
colgo i frutti del giorno
e li raduno. Allineati
su filari paralleli corrono i pensieri,
tracce di accorti innesti.
La mia vita è legata
al frugale raccolto,
il suo consumo è quotidiano, dimesso.
Nessuna logica è nel prendere
i fiori o i frutti secchi. L'unica,
e può bastare, è in questa secrezione
spontanea e vegetale dell'idea.
Lenta commozione della terra
che turbata la concepisce. O la cucina
per il suo disadorno commensale.

Every evening, bent over...

Every evening, bent over the white
garden of pages,
I gather the fruits of the day
and muster them. Thoughts run
aligned in parallel rows,
traces of subtle grafts.
My life depends
on this frugal harvest,
its daily consumption is modest.
There is no logic in choosing
dry fruits or flowers. The only one,
and it may suffice, is in this spontaneous
and vegetal secretion of the idea.
Slow stirring of the earth
that, disturbed, gives birth to it. Or cooks it
for its unadorned guest.

È specialmente nel pianto...

È specialmente nel pianto

che l'anima manifesta

la sua presenza

e per una segreta compressione

tramuta in acqua il dolore.

La prima gemmazione dello spirito

è dunque nella lacrima,

parola trasparente e lenta.

Secondo questa elementare alchimia

veramente il pensiero si fa sostanza

come una pietra o un braccio.

E non c'è turbamento nel liquido,

ma solo minerale

sconforto della materia.

1980

The soul manifests...

The soul manifests

its presence

especially in weeping

and by secret compression

turns sorrow into water.

The first budding of the spirit

is therefore in a tear,

slow and transparent word.

According to this elemental alchemy

thought truly becomes substance

like a stone or an arm.

And there's no agitation in the liquid,

only the mineral

discomfort of matter.

1980

Ho finalmente imparato...

Ho finalmente imparato
a leggere la viva
costellazione delle donne
e degli uomini le linee
che uniscono tra loro le figure.
E ora m'accorgo dei cenni
che legano il disordine del cielo.

In questa volta disegnata dal pensiero
distinguo la rotazione della luce
e l'oscillare dei segni.

Così si chiude il giorno
mentre passeggio
nel silenzioso orto degli sguardi.

1980

At last I've learned...

At last I've learned

to read the live

constellation of women and men

the lines uniting

figures among themselves.

Now I perceive the hints

that bind the disorder of the sky.

In this vault drawn by thought

I distinguish the light's rotation

and the wavering of signs.

So the day ends

with me sauntering

in the silent garden of glances.

1980

Uno vicino all'altro...

Uno vicino all'altro dopo il pasto

stanno i bicchieri degli sposi, congiunti

in una adiacenza nuziale.

Ovunque, contagiando

vestiti e suppellettili

la coppia tradisce il suo passaggio

e lascia dietro di sé

cose abbinate, pari, toccantisi

tra loro, testimoni,

paia del mondo.

1987

One next to the other...

One next to the other after the meal
stand the newlyweds' glasses, linked
in a nuptial proximity.
Everywhere, tarnishing
clothes and furniture
the couple reveals its passage
and leaves behind things
joined, matching, paired,
witnesses,
duplicates of the world.

1987

GIORGIO GUGLIELMINO

Giorgio Guglielmino was born in Genoa in 1957. In 1984 he began his career as a diplomat, working with such countries as Great Britain, Kenya, and Argentina. Interested in contemporary art, he is a collector and for a while coowned an art gallery in Milan. His poetry has been published in many periodicals, including *Tam Tam*, *Anterem*, *Barbablù* and *Discorso diretto* ("Direct Discourse"). Among his collections of poems are *Albero genealogico* (1976; "Family Tree"), *Poesie-Tatuaggio* (1982; "Tattoo Poems"), and *Poesie impossibili* (1988; "Impossible Poems"). He is also a prolific art critic, and his two studies, *Le opere d'arte trafugate: Legislazione e normativa internazionale* (1997; "Stolen Art Work: International Legislation and Regulation") and *Come guardare l'arte contemporanea e vivere felice* (2000; "How to Look at Contemporary Art and Live Happily"), are widely read. He currently resides in London. His combined interest in visual poetry and transcendent language is apparent in *Poesie di carta* (1991; "Paper Poems"), in which poems such as "Bella bellissima" ("Haunting Divine") subtly combine written word and image. The idioms that make up the poem are transposed and manipulated in the accompanying representation.

senza punteggiatura...

senza punteggiatura la sua casa è una lingua prediletta

e la sua voce è così bella da sembrare azzurra

non ha più fiato eppure parla parole ancora belle

è una donna che nuota ed ora è a riva quasi a riva

without punctuation...

without punctuation his house

is a beloved idiom

his voice as beautiful as dark blue enamel

he has no breath left yet

he speaks sweet cadenced words

a woman swimming now ashore almost ashore

e si tende questo senso estremo...

e si tende questo senso estremo tra una parola e l'altra

sembra spezzare la grana dell'inchiostro e della voce

è così che come un segno inquieto il senso si divora

e i suoni sono nuvole ferme sulla pianura della carta

and utmost meaning flexes...

and utmost meaning flexes between words

cleaving the pith of ink and voice

thus sense—a harried sign—devours itself

and sounds are clouds stock-still on paper plains

bella bellissima...

bella bellissima questa poesia piena di lontananza e cielo

dove le parole non lasciano respiro al senso

dove la notte è carta che assorbe le vocali nere

che sulla pelle non avranno più dettaglio alcuno

haunting divine...

haunting divine

this poem full of distances and sky

where words won't let sense breathe

where night is paper

sucking black vowels in

that on the skin

lose their details

Permissions

Permission to include Italian poems and to translate them in this volume has been granted by the following publishers, authors, or heirs:

Adelphi Edizioni: Cristina Campo, "Ora rivoglio bianche tutte le mie lettere," "Devota come ramo"—from *La tigre assenza* © 1991 Adelphi Edizioni.

Alfredo de Palchi: "Orecchio il silenzio di quella sedia," "Sono il dilemma," "Quanto usufruire dello spasimo"—from *Paradigma* (Caramanica Editore, 2001).

Anterem Edizioni: Giorgio Guglielmino, "senza punteggiatura la sua casa," "e si tende questo senso estremo tra una parola," "bella bellissima questa poesia"; Anna Malfaiera, "Ho spesso," "Siamo al grado zero."

Casa Editrice Rocco Carabba s.r.l.: Umberto Saba, "Teatro degli Artigianelli"—from *Parole*, 1934.

Fondazione Istituto Gramsci: Sibilla Aleramo, "Son tanto brava"—from *Selva d'amore*.

Luigi Fontanella: "Quattro barche di pescatori," "Quando ad un tratto si fa strada," "Hegira" (Caramanica Editore).

Livia Fortini: Franco Fortini, "Prologo ai vicini," "Giardino d'Estate, Pechino."

Garzanti Libri s.p.a.: Carlo Betocchi, "E ne dondola il ramo," "A cuci e scuci," "Un passo, un altro passo"—from *Tutte le poesie*, Garzanti Editore s.p.a.; Giorgio Caproni, "Il gibbone," "Interludio," "L'ora"—from *Tutte le poesie*, Garzanti Libri s.p.a., 1999; Mario Luzi, "Pur che," "Versi dal monte," "E il lupo," "Poscritto," "Senior"—from *Tutte le poesie*, Garzanti Libri s.p.a., 2001; Pier Paolo Pasolini, "Le ceneri di Gramsci"—from *Le ceneri di Gramsci*, Garzanti Libri s.p.a., Milano, 1999, 2003; Pier Paolo Pasolini, "Al sole"—from *La religione del mio tempo*, Garzanti Libri s.p.a., Milano, 1999, 2001, 2005; Sandro Penna, "Fanciullo, non fuggire, non andare," "Salgono in compagnia dei genitori," "È l'ora in cui si baciano i marmocchi"—from *Poesie*, Garzanti Libri s.p.a., Milano, 2000; Antonia Pozzi,

"La porta che si chiude," "Presagio"—from *Parole*, Garzanti Libri s.p.a., Milano, 1998, 2001; Amelia Rosselli, "Lo sdrucciolo cuore che in me è ribelle," "Mio angelo, io non seppi mai quale"—from *Le poesie*, Garzanti Editore s.p.a., 1997; Camillo Sbarbaro, "Taci, anima mia. Son questi i tristi," "Versi a Dina," "Ora che sei venuta"—from *L'opera in versi e in prosa*, Garzanti Editore s.p.a., 1985, 1995; Garzanti Libri s.p.a., 1999.

Dr. F. A. Govoni: Corrado Govoni, "Cavallo"—from *Canzoni a bocca chiusa*; "Siepe"—from *Pellegrino d'amore*; "Palazzo dell'anima"—from *Gli aborti*.

Alfredo Giuliani: "I giorni aggrappati alla città"—from *Il cuore zoppo* (Varese: Magenta, 1955).

Anita Sanesi Guarino: Roberto Sanesi, "Anniversario," "Occhi di pane azzimo ha la luna"—from *Poesie per Athikte* (Luigi Maestri Editore, Milano, 1959).

Valerio Magrelli c/o Agenzia letteraria Internazionale s.r.l.: Valerio Magrelli, "Ogni sera chino sul chiaro," "È specialmente nel pianto," "Ho finalmente imparato"—from *Ora serrata retinae* © copyright Valerio Magrelli, all rights reserved, published in Italy by Giangiacomo Feltrinelli Editore, Milano; Valerio Magrelli, "Uno vicino all'altro dopo il pasto"—from *Nature e venature* © copyright Valerio Magrelli, all rights reserved, published in Italy by Giulio Einaudi Editore, Torino.

Arnoldo Mondadori s.p.a.: Milo De Angelis, "Per quell' innato scatto-Semifinale," from *Biografia sommaria* © 1999 Arnoldo Mondadori Editore s.p.a., Milano; Milo De Angelis, "Sala parto," *Distante un padre* © 1989 Arnoldo Mondadori Editore s.p.a., Milano; Vincenzo Cardarelli, "Saluto di stagione," "Estiva"— from *Poesie* © 1947 Arnoldo Mondadori Editore, Milano; Eugenio Montale, "Valmorbia," "Portami il girasole ch'io lo trapianti," "Meriggiare pallido e assorto," "Avrei voluto sentirmi scabro ed essenziale," "Ho sostato talvolta nelle grotte," "Scirocco"—from *Ossi di seppia* © 1948 Arnoldo Mondadori Editore, Milano; Eugenio Montale, "L'altro"—from *Satura* © 1971 Arnoldo Mondadori Editore, Milano; Aldo Palazzeschi, "Il ritratto di Corinna Spiga," "Visita alla Contessa Eva"—from *Poesie* © Arnoldo Mondadori, Milano; Aldo Palazzeschi, "Rue du